COOKBOOK UK

Affordable & Flavourful Air Fryer Recipes and Step-By-Step Guide for Beginners | Healthy and Delicious Meals for Family and the Solitary | Full-color Edition

Ellie Peacock

© Copyright 2023
- All Rights Reserved

This document is geared towards providing exact and reliable information concerning the topic and issue covered. In no way is it legal to reproduce, duplicate, or transmit any part of this document in either electronic means or printed format. Recording this publication is strictly prohibited. Any storage of this document is not allowed unless with written permission from the publisher.

All rights reserved. The information provided herein is stated to be truthful and consistent, in that any liability, in terms of inattention or otherwise, by any usage or abuse of any policies, processes, or directions contained within is the solitary and utter responsibility of the recipient reader.

Under no circumstances will any legal responsibility or blame be held against the publisher for any reparation, damages, or monetary loss due to the information herein, either directly or indirectly. Respective authors own all copyrights not held by the publisher.

The information herein is offered for informational purposes solely and is universal as so. The presentation of the information is without a contract or any type of guarantee assurance. The trademarks used are without any consent, and the publication of any trademark is without permission or backing by the trademark owner.

All trademarks and brands within this book are for clarifying purposes only, are owned by the owners themselves, and are not affiliated with this document.

Contents

Introduction	01

Fundamentals of Air Fryer 02

What is an Air Fryer?	02
Benefits of Using It	03
Tips to Prepare Healthy Foods in Air Fryer	03
Step-By-Step of Air Frying	04
Tips for Using Accessories	05
Straight from the Store	05
Cleaning and Caring for Your Air Fryer	06
Frequently Asked Questions & Notes	06

4-Week Meal Plan 07

Week 1	07
Week 2	07
Week 3	08
Week 4	08

Chapter 1 Breakfast Recipes 09

Fluffy Cheese Scones	09
Creamy Fried Squid and Egg Yolks	09
Vanilla Pumpkin Bread	10
Walnut Banana Muffins	10
Orange Blueberry Muffins	11
Scrambled Eggs with Tomatoes	11
Scrambled Egg with Fresh Mushrooms	12
Breakfast Yoghurt Carrot Muffins	12
Vanilla Chocolate Banana Bread	13
Eggy Bread	13
Cloud Eggs on Toast	14
Scottish Oats Porridge with Blueberries	14
Caramel Chocolate Crumpets with Walnut Praline	15
English Breakfast Potato Frittata	15
Pumpkin Scones	16

Chapter 2 Snack and Appetizer Recipes ... 17

Crispy Air fried Potatoes and Asparagus	17
Cheese Eggplant Rolls	17
Pesto Egg and Cherry Tomato Muffins	18
Chocolate and Pear Flapjacks	18
Cheesy Hash Brown Casserole	19
Mini Cheese Chorizo Frittatas	19
Lemon Cream Scones	20
Mini Crumpets Pizza	20
Mini Bean and Sausage Pies with Cheese	21
Cheesy Apple and Potato Pasties	21
Golden Prawn Balls	22
Puff Pastry Pigs in a Blanket	22
Crispy Honey Mustard Halloumi Bars	23
Cinnamon Apple Crisps	23
Sticky Beef Bites	24
Parmesan Carrot Fries	24
Grilled Zucchini Cheese Rolls	25

Chapter 3 Vegetable and Sides Recipes ... 26

Roasted Cheese Garlic Dip	26
Chili Parsnip and Cauliflower Soup	26
Cream and Cheese Stuffed Pumpkin	27
Tomatoes-Stuffed Peppers with Cheese	27
Easy British Mackerel Fillets	28
Roasted Vegetables with Herbs	28
Cheese Vegetable Pie	29
Roasted Vegetables and Stilton Soup	29
Crispy Spicy Oysters	30
Green Asparagus Soup	30
Rosemary Vegetable Soup	31
Creamy Cauliflower Potato Soup	31

Cream Carrot Soup with Pancetta Bread ... 32

Chapter 4 Fish and Seafood Recipes 33

Fried Oysters with Cheesy Garlic Butter ... 33
Air Fryer Herbed Salmon 33
Marinated Lime Salmon 34
Roasted Cajun Salmon 34
Honey Glazed Salmon 35
Salmon with Tomato Beans Salad 35
Crispy Cod 36
Crispy Tilapia Fillets 36
Easy Air Fryer Salmon 37
Garlicky Cod Loins 37
Crispy Anchovies with Lemon 38
Air Fryer Lemon Mackerel Fillets 38
Air Fryer Kalamansi Tilapia 39
Baked Lemony Rainbow Trout 39

Chapter 5 Chicken and Poultry Recipes ... 40

Chicken Wings with Blue Cheese Dressing 40
Spicy Chicken Wings 40
Honey Mustard Glazed Chicken Wings 41
Spicy Butterfly Chicken Drumsticks 41
Air Fryer Curry Chicken Drumsticks 42
Spiced Chicken with Bird's Eye Chilies...... 42
Simple Turkey Steaks 43
Crispy Turkey Escalope 43
Crispy Parmesan Turkey Cutlets 44
Crispy Breaded Chicken Breasts 44
Cheese Turkey Meatballs 45
Air Fryer Chicken Meatballs 45
Garlicky Turkey Breast with Herbs 46
Paprika Chicken Thighs 46
Easy Air Fryer Chicken Breasts 47
Air Fryer Spiced Chicken with Vegetables ... 47
Spiced Whole Duck 48
Chicken and Veggie Skewers 48
Chicken-Avocado Patties 49
Cumin Boneless Chicken Thighs 49

Chapter 6 Beef, Pork and Lamb Recipes ... 50

Easy Beef Burgers 50
Herbed Steak Bites 50
Air Fryer Steaks with Sweet Potatoes & Mushrooms 51
Easy Air Fryer Porterhouse Steaks 51
Pork Belly with Golden Syrup Sauce 52
Tasty Rib-Eye Steak 52
Sweet & Sour Flank Steak 53
Homemade Beef Jerky 53
Mustard Pork Chops with Potatoes........... 54
Herb Roast Beef 54
Air Fryer Mustard Pork Tenderloin 55
Simple Pork Steaks 55
Easy Air Fryer Lamb Steaks 56
Delicious Marinated Pork Chops 56
Herbed Lamb Ribs 57
Macadamia Crusted Rack of Lamb........... 57
Herbed Lamb Chops with Garlic Sauce 58
Rack of lamb with Mint Pesto 58

Chapter 7 Dessert Recipes 59

Pear, Blackberry and Pistachio Crumble ... 59
Raspberry Cupcakes 59
Maple Pears with Roasted Pecan Nuts 60
Banana Bread with Vanilla Ricotta & Raspberries Compote 60
Apple Hazelnut Cookies 61
Toffee Apple Bread with Cream Pudding ... 61
Orange and Lemon Tangy Pie 62
Hazelnut Cookies 62
Traditional Cranachan......................... 63
Banana Cake 63
Coconut Cherry Pie 64
Easy Gingerbread Bundt Cake 64
Fluffy Orange Soufflé 65
Pumpkin Pecan Muffins 65

Conclusion 66

Appendix Recipes Index 67

Introduction

Welcome to a world where hot air transforms simple ingredients into crispy delights! The realm of air frying is not as new as one might imagine. Journey back a few decades, and you'll find the origins of air frying rooted in Western Europe. The promise? Delivering the beloved crispness of fried foods with less to no oil, creating a revolutionary way to savor our favorites while sidelining some of the guilt.

An air fryer is a revolutionary kitchen appliance designed to produce crispy dishes without immersing them in oil. Yes, you heard it right - the oil. Since its debut in 2010, this appliance has graced countless kitchens globally, with its popularity only poised to expand.

Fast forward to today, and this kitchen gadget has danced its way into hearts and homes across the globe. From the bustling streets of New York to the tranquil towns of New Zealand, the air fryer is not just a passing trend—it's become a countertop mainstay. Its growing popularity isn't merely due to its promise of healthier meals; the efficiency, versatility, and sheer joy of experimentation have made it an indispensable tool in the modern kitchen.

While many may perceive the air fryer as a mere frying tool, its culinary catalog extends far beyond. From frying to roasting, grilling to baking, this versatile device easily crafts delectable dishes. The secret? Its "Rapid Air Technology" circulates hot air with precision, replicating the effect of submerging food in a hot oil bath.

The standout feature? It can use almost 80% less of the cooking oil. Plus, the speed is unmatched – meals are ready in a fraction of the conventional time. A cooking game-changer, indeed.

Fundamentals of Air Fryer

We must understand this unique world of air frying using hot air currents! Picture this: a kitchen where the traditional frying undergoes a futuristic twist, coming up with crunchy delicacies without the greasy results. The air fryer isn't just a tool; it's an experience, a journey of flavors waiting to be unveiled. This chapter explores its design to the ballet of hot air inside, a gadget that has redefined the art of frying foods.

What is an Air Fryer?

Imagine enjoying your favorite crispy treats cooked with hot air instead of plenty of oil. Then comes the air fryer, the kitchen magician who has been redefining the art of frying for countless food enthusiasts. The appliance uses the principles of convection, where a mechanical fan directs hot air to circulate and cook the ingredients within the chamber. It still cooks amazing foods using the Maillard effect, named after the French chemist Louis-Camille Maillard, who unveiled its secrets in 1912. This reaction between reducing sugars and amino acids gives foods like seared steaks, cookies, and pan-fried meat their signature flavors and tantalizing aromas.

Remarkably, the air fryer achieves these results using less to no oil, circulating hot air at temperatures as high as 392° F. It graciously trims down oil content by an impressive 80%, making the results a healthy option. Outfitted with user-friendly features, from timer adjustments to precise temperature controls, each brand usually comes with a basket on a drip tray, ensuring minimal mess.

The appliance serves you well, especially when using it at home. When it comes to many people, the same technique will apply, but you set your ingredients in specialized air crisper trays and use a convection oven to cook. They both use similar cooking techniques, and the air fryer has a principle of crispy perfection with minimal oil. What are some of the unique features of the device?

Travel-friendly Design (portable): Your new air fryer isn't just an appliance; it's a portable kitchen companion. Whether moving from cabinet to countertop or even a trip to a friend's house for a cooking expedition, its design ensures seamless transitions.

Precision Temperature Regulation: Say goodbye to guesswork! With automatic temperature control, your meals reach consistent perfection. Adjust to your desired temperature, and the fryer ensures your dish always hits that sweet spot.

User-Friendly Digital Interface: Cooking skills or not, your air fryer doesn't discriminate. Thanks to its intuitive digital touch screen, you are in for a special experience. Regardless of the model, a few taps on the panel stand between you and an amazing dish.

Alert System: Overcooked meals? A thing of the past! With the integrated timer and buzzer, you'll always be in the know. These timely audio signals mean you can relax while your fryer does its thing, alerting you when meal perfection is achieved.

Effortless Cooking with Presets: The appliance comes with some cooking presets, easing your work in the kitchen. Your air fryer comes pre-loaded with settings for popular dishes. Select, start, and sit back - your fryer knows the drill!

Is frying without oil achievable?

Can you truly achieve that crispy goodness without drenching food in excessive oil? This question is challenging to answer because oil is more than just a cooking medium. It's a flavor enhancer, a texture transformer, and the secret sauce to many recipes. Yes, certain meals, particularly meats like poultry, occasionally require a touch of oil to get the best flair. However, the air fryer has amazing considerations with a minimalistic approach to oil. Many recipes you prepare will need mere spritzes from a cooking spray or a thin mist from an oil mister. Gone are the days of foods deep-fried in cups of oil!

Interestingly, the art of frying without excessive oil is anchored in the Maillard reaction (explained in the previous paragraphs above). It is a chemical reaction where proteins and sugars, under heat's influence,

get transformed to acquire rich flavors, tantalizing aromas, and a pleasant crispness. To achieve the Maillard magic:
- **Heat:** Central to the Maillard ballet, performance is realized at temperatures of 300°F (≈148°C) and higher, leading to that golden-brown appeal. Oil is not a prerequisite, but ensure your ingredients do not contain excessive moisture.
- **Moisture:** There is a zone of hydration that suits well for this Maillard reaction. Too damp may prevent browning; overly dry, and you end up with a charred outcome. Since air fryers use hot air circulation, moisture content should be balanced.
- **Time:** Carefully play around with the timing; extending the cooking duration at lower temperatures can yield similar Maillard marvels. With prolonged cooking time, there is a gradual release of excess moisture while progressively building the necessary heat.

Benefits of Using It

Come closer if you're still wondering about the perks of welcoming this gadget appliance to your kitchen. Let's explore the whole art of air frying and unearth the myriad treasures it holds:
A healthier horizon with the use of less oil
Wave goodbye to calories that come with the use of excessive oil. With the air fryer, you're venturing into a realm of eating without much heavy weight of guilt. Lavish pools of oil become relics of the past. Achieve that golden crunch with a mere mist of oil, cutting down fats by up to 80%. Using the air fryer system eliminates unhealthy oils, and you can comfortably enjoy your fries/chips. Your waistline and heart send their thanks!

Time is Truly on Your Side
Modern life is full of busy schedules and may call for efficiency, and the air fryer answers. Witness the marvel of dishes being ready in nearly half the time of traditional methods. Every minute saved is another savory bite or a moment with loved ones. An air fryer does not require the user to always remain alert during cooking. All you need to do is to set the temperature and cooking time and only return occasionally to shake the fryer basket for uniform cooking.

A Versatile Appliance
The gadget is amazing at achieving a symphony of dishes! From crispy fries to succulent chicken, delightful pastries to roasted veggies, its range is vast and varied. Whether you're preparing breakfast, lunch, dinner, or a midnight snack, the air fryer plays the perfect tune. You can gracefully transition into baking, grilling, or broiling roles.

Safe and Sound
You are now safe in your kitchen. No more of the unnecessary splattering of oil and potential burns. Enclosed and automated, the air fryer ensures your experience is safe, reducing the risks associated with traditional frying.

Easy Cleanup
The grand finale? Who doesn't like having less to deal with once you have enjoyed a delicious meal? The air fryer ensures that you have a kitchen devoid of greasy aftermath. The drip collection basket in

the air fryer collects whatever small amount of oil n is released while cooking. All residue oil is collected in the drip basket, and cleaning this basket ensures complete cleaning of the cooking place after the cooking is done. Most components are dishwasher-friendly, turning the tedious task of cleaning into a swift task. Most people find it easy to clean the components under a running tap.

Push, Play, and Relish
The air fryer is user-friendly. Gone are the days of hovering over sizzling pans. With intuitive controls, the air fryer is your kitchen friend. Set time and temperature depending on the recipe, press the start button, and let the culinary magic unfurl. This is also a farewell to oil splatters and unexpected burns!

Convenient to use
You use electricity to run the air fryers, and you can easily place the fryer in any convenient place in the house, plug it into the nearest electricity source, and start enjoying hassle-free cooking. Being a very compact device, it is easy to maneuver to the desired place and equally easy to operate.

Consistent Flavorful Fiesta
Don't be fooled by its scant oil use. Always expect a harmonious blend of flavors and textures each time you get in the kitchen. With precise temperature controls and even air circulation, the dishes you prepare are consistently delectable, making every meal a standing ovation. You will always achieve the fried taste and texture.

Odor-Free Cooking
One distinct advantage is the absence of that lingering fried aroma. Your kitchen stays fresh-smelling even after cooking.

Withstanding heavy cooking
Whether you're cooking for a daily meal or a feast, its robust design seamlessly handles light and heavy-duty cooking.

Durability
Crafted with durable metal and premium-grade plastic, it's about performance and longevity.

Pocket-friendly cooking and energy efficiency
Air fryers are considerably less expensive. Several models are available, and you can easily select one that meets your needs. Air fryers also run on electricity, meaning they are environmentally friendly and save you on electric bills since they are efficient in using energy.

Tips to Prepare Healthy Foods in Air Fryer

1. You can easily cook vegetables in an Air Fryer. To enjoy the best experience, soak veggies, especially harder ones. Set to soak in cold water for 20 minutes. Use a kitchen towel to dry them afterward.
2. Try out air roasting to prepare some of your winter favorites
3. At halfway of your cooking duration, it is advisable to flip or shake your foods. This ensures uniform or even browning or crisping.
Also, do a Mid-Cook Oil Spritz. Spraying a light oil mist on most foods halfway through cooking enhances the result. This is particularly true for coated foods or to cover any lingering flour patches.

Fundamentals of Air Fryer | 03

4. Read the manual before you decide to bake recipes that call for that.
5. All recipes are designed for the different air fryer models. So ensure you cook until you attain the desired doneness. If more time is needed, adjust the time accordingly since some ingredients may vary in firmness and size.
6. Be careful with the cooking time since it may vary with the specific model of the air fryer, size of ingredients or people to serve, pre-preparation of food, and many other factors.
Shorter cooking cycles may require you to preheat your air fryer for 4 minutes since you will need to increase the cooking time by 4 minutes if you set your ingredients in a cold air fryer basket.
7. Brush your food and cooking basket using good quality oil spray to ensure that you don't experience difficulties during the cleaning process.
8. Avoid Aerosol Sprays. Brands like Pam, while convenient, can harm your air fryer's container due to mismatched chemical interactions, leading to chipping.
9. Avoid Crowding your air fryer. For that perfect crispy finish, refrain from overloading your air fryer. Overcrowding prevents even air circulation. Either cook in batches or consider a larger device for bigger meals.
10. The Pause and Resume. On opening the basket mid-cook, the air fryer may pause, but it'll resume once the basket is replaced.
11. When frying very fatty foods, white smoke might emerge. Add a couple of tablespoons of water to the container base to counter this. Alternatively, a bread slice at the base can absorb excess grease, especially when cooking items like bacon.
12. Beware of Lightweight Foods. Given the robust fan in many air fryers, lightweight items can get tossed around. Ensure these items are secured or consider ways to prevent them from flying and clogging the fan.
13. When it comes to meats, accuracy is crucial. Invest in a good quality thermometer to ensure perfectly cooked proteins every time.

Step-By-Step of Air Frying

Ah, so you've decided to work with the air fryer, a modern innovation promising to revolutionize your kitchen experience! Just like mastering any new dance, getting in step with your air fryer requires a rhythm, a touch of grace, and passion. Let's see the steps:

The Warm-Up
Unbox and Admire: Gently remove the unit and accessories from the box, admiring its sleek design and curves. Familiarize yourself with its buttons, basket, and any accompanying accessories.
Clean all washable parts and pieces of the air fryer that will handle your food. Accomplishing this before storage speeds up your recipe preparation when ready to start.

Find Your Space
Positioning: Ensure you position your air fryer on a flat surface or countertop, preferably away from any wall or appliance. Give it room to breathe without stuffing it along with other things!

Preparing to Cook
• Moisture Watch: For that impeccable crisp, ensure any excess moisture, especially from marinated meats or naturally watery foods like potatoes, is thoroughly patted away.
• The Oil Equation: While the air fryer champions minimal oil use, certain foods might benefit from a touch. If you opt out of oil, a spritz of non-stick cooking spray on the food or basket can be your shield against stickiness.
• Uniformity Matters: Aim for consistent sizes in your cut ingredients when prepping your ingredients. This isn't just culinary aesthetics; it's about ensuring every part cooks uniformly.
• Clean Slate: Before the cooking process begins, ensure no leftover residue or fat drippings from prior uses. This prevents unnecessary spattering and potential smoky messes.
• You may decide to use aluminum foil for easy cleaning.
• Give Them Space: Avoid overcrowding the ingredients, allowing them ample space for hot air to circulate, even if it means multiple showtimes (or batches). Such will achieve proper and even cooking.
• Preheating: If your model has a preheat function, it's fantastic! If not, preheat. Just as a musician tunes their instrument, preheat the air fryer to the desired temperature for about 3-5 minutes, setting the stage for the culinary experience ahead.

During the Cooking Process
• Recipe Flexibility: Remember, provided recipes and their cooking times are more guidelines than strict rules. Your ingredients might vary in size, or perhaps you've tailored quantities to your liking. Additionally, 'perfectly done' is subjective and varies from one person to another. Therefore, be prepared to adjust cooking times slightly based on these variables. The density of food inside the fryer can also affect its cooking duration.
• Set the desired temperature for different recipes
• Intermission Act: As you reach the midpoint of your cooking process, it's time for a little rotation. For bite-sized ingredients like fries, a gentle basket shake will do. For the main or larger portions, like a juicy steak or a fillet of fish, turn them over to ensure an even performance.

After Cooking
• Checking Doneness: As the timer nears its end, check out the inside. Depending on your dish, you might be looking for a golden-brown finish or a certain softness.
• Remove the basket from the drawer before you get hold of your food.
• Use the collected juices for preparing delicious sauces and marinades
• Unplug the unit from the wall unit, allow it to cool, and clean the basket and drawer for next use.

Always Remember
The air fryer isn't just a kitchen gadget; it's a portal to culinary adventures. While it's known for recreating traditional fried delights, its capabilities don't stop there. This guide will take you beyond the conventional, showcasing the diverse dishes waiting to be discovered. View this great device as a canvas for healthy, creative cookery. From frying to roasting, steaming to baking, let your imagination and this air fryer transform your kitchen escapades into delicacies of flavors and textures.

The Different Functions
Your air fryer arrives neatly packed, complete with an instruction manual

ensuring easy assembly. Some brands come with a recipe booklet.
When the itch to cook strikes and you have your ingredients lined up, just pop them into the basket and slide them into the fryer. Some recipes might prompt you to give your fryer a quick preheat. With the basket snugly in place, dial in your desired temperature and set your timer. Then, let the culinary magic commence.

Here's a glimpse into the multifaceted cooking styles your air fryer can effortlessly execute:

1. Fry

Step 1: **Preheat Prelude** - Begin by warming up your air fryer to the desired temperature. Most dishes thrive at a temperature range of 350°F to 400°F.
Step 2: **Oil Spray** - Lightly coat your chosen ingredients with a touch of oil or cooking spray. This ensures a crispy, golden exterior.
Step 3: **Ingredients in the Basket** - Place the ingredients in the basket, ensuring they have space to rotate. Crowding might lead to an uneven fry.
Step 4: **Mid-way shake** - Halfway through, gently shake the basket to rotate ingredients, ensuring a consistent golden hue.
Step 5: End - Once your ingredients have rotated to crispy perfection, carefully remove them. Serve immediately for the best crunch!

2. Roast

Step 1: **Preheating** - Preheat the air fryer to the roasting temperature, typically between 325°F to 375°F.
Step 2: **Seasoned Performance** - Season your chosen ingredients. For vegetables, a drizzle of oil, salt, and pepper might serve well. Meats might require a more extensive marinade or rub.
Step 3: **Set Ingredients** - Place your ingredients in the basket, ensuring even spacing for a uniform roast.
Step 4: **Rotate & Revel** - Midway, turn the ingredients to ensure all sides get their moment under the hot air.
Step 5: **Final stage** - Once roasted to your desired level, remove and let the dish cool briefly before serving.

3. Bake

Step 1: **Initial Preheating** - Preheat the air fryer to your baking temperature. This could vary based on the dish but is often between 300°F to 350°F.
Step 2: **Preparation Solo** - Prepare your batter or dough as per your recipe.
Step 3: **Mold & Set** - If you're using a mold or pan (like for muffins or cakes), ensure it's air fryer compatible. Fill it up and place it inside.
Step 4: **Bake & Wait** - Let the ingredients bake. Resist the urge to peek too often.
Step 5: **Final stage** - Once baked to perfection, remove, let it cool slightly, and then enjoy your airy and fluffy bake!

4. Grill

Step 1: **Tuning and Preheating** - Preheat the air fryer to a high temperature, usually around 400°F, similar to grilling conditions.
Step 2: **Marination** - Prepare your meats or vegetables by marinating or seasoning them.
Step 3: **Basket Brilliance** - Place the ingredients in the basket. For an authentic grill feel, you can use an air fryer grill pan if you have one.
Step 4: **Mid-grill Maneuver** - Halfway through, flip your ingredients

for even grill marks and cooking.
Step 5: **Final Stages** - Once grilled to your satisfaction, remove the dish, allow it to cool for a few minutes, and then enjoy!

Tips for Using Accessories

While the fryer can certainly work well on its own, adding accessories gives you amazing results! Here are some of the accessories.

1. Air Fryer Basket: Ensure it's clean and dry before each use. When cooking, give ingredients ample space for that golden crisp finish.
2. Air Fryer Baking Pan: Ideal for muffins, cakes, and bread. Lightly grease before pouring in the batter to ensure nothing sticks.
3. Air Fryer Double Layer Rack: When one layer isn't enough! Ensure even spacing on both levels for uniform cooking.
4. Air Fryer Grill Pan: Perfect for that grilled finish on meats and veggies. Clean those grooves post-use for an optimum grilling experience.
5. Air Fryer Food Separator: Cooking fries and chicken together? Keep flavors distinct with this tool. One on the left and the other on the right.
6. Cooking Oil Filter: Use this to ensure your oil is free from particles, especially if reusing.
7. Charcoal Barbecue Filter: Replace regularly to keep any smoky or lingering odors at bay.
8. Lift Lid: A safer way to check on your food without pausing the cooking process.
9. Bamboo Cutting Board: A sustainable choice for prepping when you need to cut your ingredients. Remember to clean and dry after each use.
10. Frying Pan Cover: Keeps your countertop clean by catching any unexpected splashes or pops.
11. Cookie Sheet Liners: Perfect for keeping delicate baked goods warm. Remember, metal cookie cutters can scratch them, so be gentle!
12. Sear Plate: For those times you crave that perfect sear on your steak or fish.
13. Removable Crumb Tray: Regularly empty and clean this tray to keep your fryer functioning flawlessly.
14. Silicone Muffin Molds: Use these for perfectly shaped muffins and cupcakes. A light grease before pouring batter ensures easy release.

Straight from the Store

The moment has arrived. Opening the packaging, revealing what promises to be your new kitchen friend: The Air Fryer. What is in the box.

The Air Fryer Unit:

Sturdy and sleek, this main unit houses the heart of your air fryer. It has an intuitive design, often fitted with digital screens and dials.

Included Accessories:

Removable Air Fryer Basket: The essential vessel, perfect for everything from crispy fries to delicate seafood.
Cooking chamber: This is where you place your food to cook. Depending

Fundamentals of Air Fryer | 05

on the brand and model, it could be a single tray or multi-tray.
We also have the convection fan, exhaust system, and heating elements.
User Manual: This isn't just a booklet; it's your guide to understanding your appliance's habits, charms, and full potential.
Warranty Card: Keep this safe.

Acquiring Ingredients: Curating Your Culinary Palette

1. Go to the Local Farmers' Markets: A treasure trove of fresh produce. Here, veggies and fruits are fresh.
2. Butchers & Fisheries: For the freshest cuts of meat and catches of the day. Remember, freshness translates to flavor.
3. Ethnic Groceries: Spice up your air fryer adventures. From Asian sesame oils to Middle Eastern spices, these stores hold the key to global cuisines.
4. Bulk Stores: For your grains, seeds, and dried fruits. It is not only economical but also eco-friendly if you bring your own containers.
5. Specialty Stores: Sometimes, a dish demands a specific ingredient, be it truffle oil or a rare cheese. Specialty stores are your go-to for these unique items.
6. Your Own Garden: Nothing beats the joy of plucking a tomato off your plant or snipping fresh herbs straight into your air fryer basket.

Cleaning and Caring for Your Air Fryer

If you don't clean and maintain the air fryer well, it won't last for long.

How to Clean Your Air Fryer:

1. Unplug the air fryer from the source of power or wall socket. Allow the appliance to cool completely.
2. Utilize a damp cloth to wipe the appliance's exterior.
3. Remove all removable parts like the air fryer pan, tray, and basket, and wash them using hot water and a dishwasher soap.
4. Take a sponge or damp cloth and clean the inner section.
5. Use a brush to scrub any ingredients that tick in the air fryer.
6. Allow all accessories to air dry before returning them to the unit.
7. Once clean, ensure you store it well.

Maintaining Your Air Fryer:

1. Check the power chord to ensure it is not damaged to avoid accidents.
2. Ensure no debris in the fryer before you start cooking.
3. Set your air fryer on a flat countertop.
4. Set it away from the wall or another gadget. Maintain a 4-inch distance to the nearest element.
5. Check all components to ensure they are in good condition.
6. I f any is damaged, let it be repaired or replaced.

Frequently Asked Questions & Notes

1. I see white or black smoke coming out of my air fryer. Should I be alarmed? White smoke typically arises from an accumulation of fat or excess oil pooling at the fryer's bottom. A quick cleaning should resolve this. Black smoke, however, signals a problem with the machine itself. In this case, immediately unplug and seek professional repair.

2. My food is not crisping. Is it an oil issue? Yes, if your food turns out dry, chewy, or lacks that golden crisp, it's likely due to insufficient oil. Remember, air frying creates a crunchy texture due to the tiny circulating oil molecules. When these are absent, you're just baking, leading to a blander outcome. Always follow the recipe's oil instructions.

3. There's a lingering smell in my air fryer. What to do? Proper cleaning post-use is your best defense against lingering odors. Soak and scrub the fryer basket and any accessories in hot, soapy water. Ensure thorough rinsing and drying before your next cooking.

4. Can I line my air fryer with baking paper or aluminum foil? While you can, be cautious. The air fryer's powerful fans might cause these linings to flutter onto the heating element, risking burns. If you must use them, perforate them for better airflow.

5. Do I need to preheat? Though not always necessary, preheating helps in achieving a consistent cooking result. If unsure, simply warm up your fryer to the desired temperature for a few minutes before introducing your ingredients.

6. Is there a risk of overloading my air fryer? Yes! Overcrowding hampers even cooking. If you're cooking for a large group, either cook in batches or consider investing in a larger air fryer.

Fundamentals of Air Fryer

4-Week Meal Plan

Week 1

Day 1:
Breakfast: Walnut Banana Muffins
Lunch: Cheese Vegetable Pie
Snack: Crispy Air fried Potatoes and Asparagus
Dinner: Easy Beef Burgers
Dessert: Pear, Blackberry and Pistachio Crumble

Day 2:
Breakfast: Pumpkin Scones
Lunch: Roasted Vegetables and Stilton Soup
Snack: Golden Prawn Balls
Dinner: Chicken Wings with Blue Cheese Dressing
Dessert: Raspberry Cupcakes

Day 3:
Breakfast: Vanilla Pumpkin Bread
Lunch: Rosemary Vegetable Soup
Snack: Cheesy Hash Brown Casserole
Dinner: Fried Oysters with Cheesy Garlic Butter
Dessert: Apple Hazelnut Cookies

Day 4:
Breakfast: Scrambled Eggs with Tomatoes
Lunch: Roasted Vegetables with Herbs
Snack: Mini Cheese Chorizo Frittatas
Dinner: Pork Belly with Golden Syrup Sauce
Dessert: Traditional Cranachan

Day 5:
Breakfast: Orange Blueberry Muffins
Lunch: Creamy Cauliflower Potato Soup
Snack: Chocolate and Pear Flapjacks
Dinner: Air Fryer Herbed Salmon
Dessert: Toffee Apple Bread with Cream Pudding

Day 6:
Breakfast: Fluffy Cheese Scones
Lunch: Green Asparagus Soup
Snack: Cinnamon Apple Crisps
Dinner: Easy Air Fryer Lamb Steaks
Dessert: Banana Bread with Vanilla Ricotta & Raspberries Compote

Day 7:
Breakfast: Scrambled Egg with Fresh Mushrooms
Lunch: Tomatoes-Stuffed Peppers with Cheese
Snack: Mini Bean and Sausage Pies with Cheese
Dinner: Spicy Butterfly Chicken Drumsticks
Dessert: Orange and Lemon Tangy Pie

Week 2

Day 1:
Breakfast: Vanilla Chocolate Banana Bread
Lunch: Roasted Cheese Garlic Dip
Snack: Lemon Cream Scones
Dinner: Herbed Steak Bites
Dessert: Banana Cake

Day 2:
Breakfast: Breakfast Yoghurt Carrot Muffins
Lunch: Chili Parsnip and Cauliflower Soup
Snack: Cheesy Apple and Potato Pasties
Dinner: Simple Turkey Steaks
Dessert: Maple Pears with Roasted Pecan Nuts

Day 3:
Breakfast: Creamy Fried Squid and Egg Yolks
Lunch: Cream Carrot Soup with Pancetta Bread
Snack: Mini Crumpets Pizza
Dinner: Salmon with Tomato Beans Salad
Dessert: Orange and Lemon Tangy Pie

Day 4:
Breakfast: Cloud Eggs on Toast
Lunch: Cream and Cheese Stuffed Pumpkin
Snack: Cinnamon Apple Crisps
Dinner: Mustard Pork Chops with Potatoes
Dessert: Hazelnut Cookies

Day 5:
Breakfast: Eggy Bread
Lunch: Roasted Vegetables and Stilton Soup
Snack: Crispy Honey Mustard Halloumi Bars
Dinner: Garlicky Cod Loins
Dessert: Fluffy Orange Soufflé

Day 6:
Breakfast: Caramel Chocolate Crumpets with Walnut Praline
Lunch: Cheese Vegetable Pie
Snack: Puff Pastry Pigs in a Blanket
Dinner: Herbed Lamb Chops with Garlic Sauce
Dessert: Coconut Cherry Pie

Day 7:
Breakfast: Scottish Oats Porridge with Blueberries
Lunch: Creamy Cauliflower Potato Soup
Snack: Grilled Zucchini Cheese Rolls
Dinner: Crispy Breaded Chicken Breasts
Dessert: Pumpkin Pecan Muffins

Week 3

Day 1:
Breakfast: English Breakfast Potato Frittata
Lunch: Rosemary Vegetable Soup
Snack: Golden Prawn Balls
Dinner: Tasty Rib-Eye Steak
Dessert: Easy Gingerbread Bundt Cake

Day 2:
Breakfast: Pumpkin Scones
Lunch: Cream Carrot Soup with Pancetta Bread
Snack: Parmesan Carrot Fries
Dinner: Cheese Turkey Meatballs
Dessert: Pear, Blackberry and Pistachio Crumble

Day 3:
Breakfast: Scrambled Eggs with Tomatoes
Lunch: Roasted Cheese Garlic Dip
Snack: Crispy Honey Mustard Halloumi Bars
Dinner: Delicious Marinated Pork Chops
Dessert: Toffee Apple Bread with Cream Pudding

Day 4:
Breakfast: Fluffy Cheese Scones
Lunch: Roasted Vegetables with Herbs
Snack: Sticky Beef Bites
Dinner: Crispy Anchovies with Lemon
Dessert: Apple Hazelnut Cookies

Day 5:
Breakfast: Vanilla Pumpkin Bread
Lunch: Tomatoes-Stuffed Peppers with Cheese
Snack: Crispy Air fried Potatoes and Asparagus
Dinner: Crispy Tilapia Fillets
Dessert: Banana Bread with Vanilla Ricotta & Raspberries Compote

Day 6:
Breakfast: Walnut Banana Muffins
Lunch: Creamy Cauliflower Potato Soup
Snack: Cinnamon Apple Crisps
Dinner: Rack of lamb with Mint Pesto
Dessert: Orange and Lemon Tangy Pie

Day 7:
Breakfast: Scrambled Eggs with Tomatoes
Lunch: Green Asparagus Soup
Snack: Cheesy Hash Brown Casserole
Dinner: Garlicky Turkey Breast with Herbs
Dessert: Traditional Cranachan

Week 4

Day 1:
Breakfast: Breakfast Yoghurt Carrot Muffins
Lunch: Chili Parsnip and Cauliflower Soup
Snack: Pesto Egg and Cherry Tomato Muffins
Dinner: Easy Air Fryer Porterhouse Steaks
Dessert: Raspberry Cupcakes

Day 2:
Breakfast: Scrambled Egg with Fresh Mushrooms
Lunch: Roasted Cheese Garlic Dip
Snack: Mini Cheese Chorizo Frittatas
Dinner: Paprika Chicken Thighs
Dessert: Pear, Blackberry and Pistachio Crumble

Day 3:
Breakfast: Orange Blueberry Muffins
Lunch: Cream Carrot Soup with Pancetta Bread
Snack: Chocolate and Pear Flapjacks
Dinner: Easy British Mackerel Fillets
Dessert: Hazelnut Cookies

Day 4:
Breakfast: Creamy Fried Squid and Egg Yolks
Lunch: Cream and Cheese Stuffed Pumpkin
Snack: Lemon Cream Scones
Dinner: Air Fryer Mustard Pork Tenderloin
Dessert: Coconut Cherry Pie

Day 5:
Breakfast: Vanilla Chocolate Banana Bread
Lunch: Roasted Vegetables and Stilton Soup
Snack: Mini Bean and Sausage Pies with Cheese
Dinner: Easy Air Fryer Lamb Steaks
Dessert: Pumpkin Pecan Muffins

Day 6:
Breakfast: Eggy Bread
Lunch: Cheese Vegetable Pie
Snack: Mini Crumpets Pizza
Dinner: Herbed Lamb Ribs
Dessert: Fluffy Orange Soufflé

Day 7:
Breakfast: Cloud Eggs on Toast
Lunch: Rosemary Vegetable Soup
Snack: Cheesy Apple and Potato Pasties
Dinner: Spiced Whole Duck
Dessert: Easy Gingerbread Bundt Cake

Chapter 1 Breakfast Recipes

Fluffy Cheese Scones

⏰ **Prep:** 15 minutes 🍴 **Cook:** 12 minutes 📚 **Serves:** 4

Ingredients:

1 cup self-raising flour, plus extra for dusting
¼ cup chilled butter, cut into cubes
1 teaspoon baking powder
pinch of salt
pinch cayenne pepper
1 cup grated cheddar cheese
¼ cup milk, plus 1 tablespoon for glazing

Preparation:

1. Switch the air fryer to 150°C and preheat for 10 minutes.
2. Sift flour, salt, baking powder and cayenne pepper in a bowl.
3. Add butter to the flour mixture and combine to form a crumbly mixture.
4. Add milk to the flour slowly and knead a firm dough.
5. Roll out the dough till 2cm-thick and cut out scones with the cookie cutter. Brush them with milk.
6. Place them in the air fryer and sprinkle grated cheese. Cook for 12 minutes until they are fluffed up and the cheese melts. Cook the rest in batches by repeating the same steps.
7. Serve warm.

Serving Suggestions: You can serve it with eggs and butter
Variation Tip: You can also use ground pepper and nutmeg for some taste variation.
Per Serving: Calories: 338 | Fat: 21.5g | Sat Fat: 13.5g | Carbohydrates: 25.6g | Fiber: 0.9g | Sugar: 0.9g | Protein: 10.9g

Creamy Fried Squid and Egg Yolks

⏰ **Prep:** 15 minutes 🍴 **Cook:** 20 minutes 📚 **Serves:** 4

Ingredients

½ cup self-rising flour
14 oz. squid, cleaned and pat dried
Salt and freshly ground black pepper
1 tablespoon olive oil
2 tablespoons butter
2 green chilies, seeded and chopped
2 curry leaves stalks
4 raw egg yolks
½ cup chicken broth
2 tablespoons evaporated milk
1 tablespoon sugar

Preparation

1. Switch the Air Fryer to 180°C. Grease an Air Fryer pan.
2. Sprinkle the squid flower evenly with salt and black pepper.
3. In a shallow dish, add the flour. Coat the squid evenly with flour and then shake off any excess flour.
4. Place the squid into the prepared pan in a single layer.
5. Air Fry for about 9 minutes.
6. Remove from the Air Fryer and set aside.
7. In a skillet heat butter and sauté the chilies and curry leaves for about 3 minutes.
8. Add the egg yolks and cook for about 1 minute, stirring continuously.
9. Gradually, add the chicken broth and cook for about 3-5 minutes, stirring continuously.
10. Add in the milk and sugar and mix until well combined.
11. Add the fried squid and toss to coat well.
12. Serve hot.

Serving Suggestions: Serve with crusted bread
Variation Tip: You can add coconut milk.
Per Serving: Calories: 311 | Fat: 16.1g | Sat Fat: 1.3g | Carbohydrates: 19.8g | Fiber: 13.7g | Sugar: 4.2g | Protein: 21g

Vanilla Pumpkin Bread

⏱ **Prep: 15 minutes** 🍳 **Cook: 25 minutes** 🍽 **Serves: 4**

Ingredients:

- ¼ cup coconut flour
- 2 tablespoons stevia blend
- 1 teaspoon baking powder
- ¾ teaspoon pumpkin pie spice
- ¼ teaspoon ground cinnamon
- ⅛ teaspoon salt
- ¼ cup canned pumpkin
- 2 large eggs
- 2 tablespoons unsweetened almond milk
- 1 teaspoon vanilla extract

Preparations:

1. In a bowl, mix together the flour, stevia, baking powder, spices, and salt.
2. In another large bowl, add the pumpkin, eggs, almond milk, and vanilla extract. Beat until well combined.
3. Then, add in the flour mixture and mix until just combined.
4. Switch the air-fryer to 175°C. Line a cake pan with greased parchment paper.
5. Place the mixture evenly into the prepared pan.
6. Arrange the pan into an air fryer basket.
7. Air fry for 25 minutes.
8. Remove the pans from the air fryer and place them onto a wire rack for about 5 minutes.
9. Carefully take out the bread from the pan and put it onto a wire rack to cool for about 5-10 minutes before slicing.
10. Cut the bread into desired-size slices and serve.

Serving Suggestions: Serve with caramel glaze
Variation Tip: You can use whole milk instead of almond milk.
Per Serving: Calories: 67 | Fat: 2.8g | Sat Fat: 1g | Carbohydrates: 9g | Fiber: 1.2g | Sugar: 6.9g | Protein: 3.5g

Walnut Banana Muffins

⏱ **Prep: 15 minutes** 🍳 **Cook: 25 minutes** 🍽 **Serves: 8**

Ingredients:

- 1½ cups plain flour
- ½ teaspoon baking soda
- ½ teaspoon baking powder
- ¼ teaspoon ground cinnamon
- 1 pinch of salt
- 2 ripe bananas, peeled and mashed
- 1 egg
- ¼ cup brown sugar
- ½ teaspoon vanilla essence
- 1½ tablespoon milk
- 2 tablespoons Nutella
- ¼ cup walnuts

Preparation:

1. Mix dry ingredients by sifting the flour, baking soda, baking powder, cinnamon, and salt.
2. Mix the remaining ingredients in another bowl except for the walnuts.
3. Add the banana mixture until just combined.
4. Fold in the walnuts.
5. Switch the Air Fryer to 120°C. Grease a muffin mold that fits in the air fryer.
6. Put the mixture evenly into the prepared muffin molds.
7. Air Fry for about 20 minutes. Check by inserting a toothpick, it should come out clean.
8. Remove the muffin molds from Air Fryer and let them cool for 10 minutes.
9. Serve.

Serving Suggestions: Serve with cream cheese.
Variation Tip: You can use chopped pecans instead of walnuts.
Per Serving: Calories: 223 | Fat: 9g | Sat Fat: 4g | Carbohydrates: 30g | Fiber: 1g | Sugar: 13g | Protein: 4g

Orange Blueberry Muffins

⏰ **Prep:** 15 minutes 🍳 **Cook:** 12 minutes 🥞 **Serves:** 12

Ingredients

- 2 cups plus 2 tablespoons self-rising flour
- ½ cup white sugar
- ½ cup milk
- 1 teaspoon vanilla extract
- 2 oz. butter, melted
- 2 eggs
- 2 teaspoons fresh orange zest, finely grated
- 2 tablespoons fresh orange juice
- ½ cup fresh blueberries

Preparation

1. Switch the Air Fryer to 180°C. Grease a muffin pan.
2. Mix flour and white sugar in a bowl.
3. In another large bowl, mix well the remaining ingredients except for the blueberries.
4. Now, add in the flour mixture and mix until just combined. Then fold in the blueberries.
5. Put the mixture evenly into the prepared muffin molds. Arrange the molds into the Air Fryer.
6. Air Fry for 12 minutes.
7. Remove the muffin molds from Air Fryer let them cool for about 10 minutes.
8. Carefully invert the muffins onto the wire rack to cool completely before serving.
9. Serve.

Serving Suggestions: Serve with coffee
Variation Tip: You can top it with blueberry sauce and buttercream.
Per Serving: Calories: 154 | Fat: 5g | Sat Fat: 1g | Carbohydrates: 23.7g | Fiber: 1g | Sugar: 6.4g | Protein: 3.7g

Scrambled Eggs with Tomatoes

⏰ **Prep:** 15 minutes 🍳 **Cook:** 11 minutes 🥞 **Serves:** 4

Ingredients

- 4 eggs
- ¾ cup milk
- Salt and freshly ground black pepper
- 8 cherry tomatoes, halved
- ½ cup Parmesan cheese, grated

Preparation:

1. Switch the air-fryer to 180°C. Grease an Air Fryer pan with cooking spray. Mix the milk, eggs, salt, and black pepper in a bowl.
2. Transfer the egg mixture to the prepared pan.
3. Air Fry for about 6 minutes until the edges begin to set.
4. With a wooden spatula, stir the egg mixture.
5. Top with the tomatoes and Air Fry for about 3 minutes or until the eggs are done.
6. Toast a slice of bread in the air-fryer for 2 minutes at 175°C.
7. Serve warm and garnish with parmesan cheese

Serving Suggestions: Serve with tea
Variation Tip: You can top it with cheddar cheese instead of parmesan
Per Serving: Calories: 341 | Fat: 17g | Sat Fat: 1g | Carbohydrates: 25.2g | Fiber: 1.2g | Sugar: 17.7g | Protein: 26.4g

Chapter 1 Breakfast Recipes | 11

Scrambled Egg with Fresh Mushrooms

🕐 **Prep:** 15 minutes 🍳 **Cook:** 10 minutes 📚 **Serves:** 2

Ingredients

4 eggs
½ cup fresh mushrooms, finely chopped
2 tablespoons unsalted butter
2 tablespoons Parmesan cheese, shredded
A pinch of salt and black pepper, to taste

Instructions

1. Switch the Air Fryer to 140°C.
2. Mix the eggs, salt, and black pepper in a bowl.
3. Grease the pan with butter.
4. Add the beaten eggs and Air Fry for about 4-5 minutes.
5. Add in the mushrooms and cook for 5 minutes, stirring occasionally.
6. Serve hot.

Serving Suggestions: Serve with parmesan cheese
Variation Tip: You can add chopped onions and bell peppers for taste variations
Per Serving:
Calories: 254 | Fat: 11g | Sat Fat: 1.1g | Carbohydrates: 2.1g | Fiber: 13.7g | Sugar: 1.4g | Protein: 12.8g

Breakfast Yoghurt Carrot Muffins

🕐 **Prep:** 15 minutes 🍳 **Cook:** 12 minutes 📚 **Serves:** 6

Ingredients

For Muffins:
¼ cup whole-wheat flour
¼ cup all-purpose flour
½ teaspoon baking powder
⅛ teaspoon baking soda
½ teaspoon dried parsley, crushed
½ teaspoon salt
½ cup yoghurt
1 teaspoon vinegar
1 tablespoon vegetable oil
3 tablespoons cottage cheese, grated
1 carrot, peeled and grated
2-4 tablespoons water (if needed)

Instructions

1. Switch the Air Fryer to 180°C. Grease 6 medium muffin molds.
2. For muffins: Mix flour, baking powder, baking soda, parsley, and salt in a bowl. Mix well the yoghurt, and vinegar along with the rest of the ingredients.
3. Place the mixture evenly into the prepared muffin molds.
4. Place the muffin molds into an Air Fryer in 2 batches.
5. Air Fry for about 12 minutes. Check by inserting a skewer. It should come out clean.
6. Remove the muffin molds from Air Fryer and let them cool for 10 minutes.
7. Carefully, invert the muffins onto the wire rack to completely cool before serving. 8. Enjoy!

Serving Suggestions: Serve by topping with sesame seeds
Variation Tip: You can add walnuts as well.
Per Serving: Calories: 222 | Fat: 12.9g | Sat Fat: 5.7g | Carbohydrates: 12.4g | Fiber: 0.9g | Sugar: 2.2g | Protein: 15.1g

Vanilla Chocolate Banana Bread

Prep: 6 minutes **Cook: 20 minutes** **Serves: 10**

Ingredients

2 cups flour
½ teaspoon baking soda
½ teaspoon baking powder
½ teaspoon salt
¾ cup sugar
⅓ cup butter, softened
3 eggs
1 tablespoon vanilla extract
1 cup milk
½ cup bananas, peeled and mashed
1 cup chocolate chips

Instructions

1. Dump in flour, baking powder, salt and baking soda and mix well. Beat sugar and butter until creamy.
2. Beat in eggs, and vanilla extract. Then, add the flour mixture and mix until well combined.
3. Add in the milk, and mashed bananas and mix them. Gently, fold in the chocolate chips.
4. Switch the Air Fryer to 180°C.
5. Grease a loaf pan and Pour the mixture into the prepared pan.
6. Arrange the loaf pan into an Air Fryer basket.
7. Air Fry for about 20 minutes.
8. Remove from Air Fryer once cooked and let it cool for 10 minutes.
9. Cut the bread into desired size slices and serve.

Serving Suggestions: Serve with butter.
Variation Tip: You can add nuts and raisins as well.
Per Serving: Calories: 333 | Fat: 13.2g | Sat Fat: 8.1g | Carbohydrates: 47.4g | Fiber: 1.5g | Sugar: 26g | Protein: 6.5g

Eggy Bread

Prep: 5 minutes **Cook: 10 minutes** **Serves: 2**

Ingredients:

2 slices white bread or brown bread
2 medium eggs
1 tablespoon milk
1 tablespoon melted butter
Oil spray
Cinnamon sugar for topping (¼ teaspoon cinnamon plus 2 teaspoons of caster sugar)

Preparation:

1. Mix all the ingredients and whisk well.
2. Dip the bread pieces in the mixture.
3. Switch the air-fryer at 160°C and preheat for 10 minutes.
4. Spray the basket with cooking spray and place the soaked bread pieces in a single layer.
5. Cook for 6 minutes, flipping halfway through to the cook time.
6. Sprinkle cinnamon sugar on top.
7. Serve warm.

Serving Suggestions: Serve with maple butter.
Variation Tip: You can also serve it with custard.
Per Serving:
Calories: 288 | Fat: 21.7g | Sat Fat: 10.4g | Carbohydrates: 10.6g | Fiber: 0.4g | Sugar: 2.2g | Protein: 13.1g

Chapter 1 Breakfast Recipes

Cloud Eggs on Toast

⏱ Prep: 10 minutes   🍲 Cook: 13 minutes   🍽 Serves: 2

Ingredients:

2 large eggs
2 tablespoons chives, chopped
Slices of sour dough bread.

Preparation:

1. Switch the air-fryer at 175°C.
2. Separate egg yolks and white.
3. Whisk egg whites with the electric beater until stiff peaks.
4. In an air fryer tray place parchment paper then scoop out a large dollop of egg white.
5. Place it in the air fryer for 8 minutes until it turns light golden.
6. Gently place an egg yolk on top of the baked egg whites. Cook in the air fryer for another 2 minutes.
7. Place carefully on the toast and garnish chopped chives.
8. Serve warm.

Serving Suggestions: Serve with baked beans
Variation Tip: You can also serve with sausages on the side as well.
Per Serving: Calories: 80 | Fat: 6g | Sat Fat: 2g | Carbohydrates: 0.3g | Fiber: 0.3g | Sugar: 0.3g | Protein: 7g

Scottish Oats Porridge with Blueberries

⏱ Prep: 5 minutes   🍲 Cook: 5 minutes   🍽 Serves: 2

Ingredients:

½ cup rolled oats
1 cup whole milk
2 tablespoons
Blueberry sauce
Pinch of salt
Fresh Blueberries for garnishing

Preparation:

1. Switch the air-fryer at 95°C and begin preheating.
2. In a small bowl that fits the air-fryer basket, add oats and the rest of the ingredients except for fresh blueberries.
3. Mix and put in the air-fryer for 3 minutes. Stir and change the side of the bowl and cook again for 2 more minutes.
4. Serve warm and garnish with blueberries.

Serving Suggestions: You can drizzle blueberry sauce and nuts.
Variation Tip: You can use plant based milk instead of whole milk.
Per Serving:
Calories: 301 | Fat: 10.6g | Sat Fat: 5g | Carbohydrates: 38.7g | Fiber: 4.1g | Sugar: 13.2g | Protein: 13.2g

| Chapter 1 Breakfast Recipes

Caramel Chocolate Crumpets with Walnut Praline

⏱ Prep: 5 minutes   🍳 Cook: 18 minutes   🍽 Serves: 2

Ingredients:

12 Golden Crumpets
¼ cup caster sugar
2 tablespoons walnuts
Pinch of salt
¼ cup dark chocolate, chopped
⅓ cup caramel sauce
⅓ cup peanut butter
2 tablespoons light cream

Preparation:

1. Switch the air fryer to 200°C.
2. Place baking paper in the air fryer tray and put walnuts. Air fryer to 3 minutes and remove from the air fryer.
3. For walnut praline: In a pan, dissolve sugar with 2 tablespoons of water on low heat until brown. Pour over roasted walnuts and set aside to cool.
4. Combine caramel with salt.
5. In a saucepan, heat the chocolate and cream and cook for 4 minutes until the chocolate is melted.
6. Switch the air fryer to 85°C and place the crumpets in the air fryer for 2 minutes.
7. Serve the crumpets on a plate, spread peanut butter, and place another crumpet over it, drizzle salted caramel sauce over it. Stack another crumpet and drizzle chocolate sauce, coarsely chop walnut praline and sprinkle over the crumpets. Make stacks of crumpets in the same manner.
8. Finally, top with fresh whipped cream.

Serving Suggestions: Serve with blueberries.
Variation Tip: You can also top it with cream cheese as well.
Per Serving: Calories:604 | Fat: 24.9g | Sat Fat: 7.5g | Carbohydrates: 83.4g | Fiber: 4.9g | Sugar: 22.6g | Protein: 16.3g

English Breakfast Potato Frittata

⏱ Prep: 10 minutes   🍳 Cook: 25 minutes   🍽 Serves: 4

Ingredients:

8 large eggs
11 oz. potato slices.
2 tablespoons olive oil
6 bacon slices, chopped
Bunch of spring onions, sliced
12 cherry tomatoes
Salt and black pepper, to taste
Handful grated Cheddar

Preparation:

1. Switch the air fryer to 200°C and preheat for 10 minutes.
2. Boil potatoes for 4 minutes on medium heat. Once cooked, drain and spread on a tea towel.
3. When they are slightly cooled, spray them with oil and pop them in the air fryer for 5 minutes. Remove once they are brown from the edges.
4. Next, add bacon slices in the air fryer and cook for 5 minutes.
5. In a baking dish, place potatoes and bacon. Add spring onions and cherry tomatoes.
6. Whisk eggs with salt and pepper and pour over the potatoes. Cover with grated cheddar cheese.
7. Pop the dish back and air fry for 7 minutes until the cheese melts and the eggs are cooked.
8. If your air fryer has a grill function, then place it under the grill for 5 minutes to set and brown the top.

Serving Suggestions: Serve with toast and relish
Variation Tip: You can also add black pudding and mushrooms.
Per Serving: Calories: 539 | Fat: g | Sat Fat: 14.1g | Carbohydrates: 16.2 g | Fiber: 4.5g | Sugar: 10.7g | Protein: 33.5g

Pumpkin Scones

Prep: 15 minutes **Cook:** 12 minutes **Serves:** 6

Ingredients:

- 3 cups self-raising flour, plus extra for rolling
- ¼ cup caster sugar
- 4 oz. cold butter
- 1 cup cooked pumpkin
- 1-2 tsp pumpkin spice
- ¼ cup milk

Preparation:

1. Switch the air fryer to 200°C and preheat for 10 minutes.
2. Mix butter, flour, sugar and pumpkin spice to form a coarse mixture.
3. Add cooked pumpkin and milk and knead the dough. If the dough is hard, you can add more milk.
4. Roll the dough and cut triangles or circles. Roll the trimmings again and repeat the same steps until all the dough is utilized.
5. Brush with the milk and place in the air fryer. Cook for 10-12 minutes until lightly brown.
6. Cook the rest of the scones in batches.
7. Dish out and serve.

Serving Suggestions: Serve with butter or cream cheese flavored frosting with a pinch of cinnamon, to serve
Variation Tip: You can use caramel topping as well.
Per Serving: Calories: 414 | Fat: 16.3g | Sat Fat: 10g | Carbohydrates: 60g | Fiber: 2.9g | Sugar: 10.3g | Protein: 7.4g

Chapter 1 Breakfast Recipes

Chapter 2 Snack and Appetizer Recipes

Crispy Air fried Potatoes and Asparagus

Prep: 10 minutes **Cook:** 30 minutes **Serves:** 6

Ingredients:

1½ lbs. Baby Potatoes, quartered
8 oz. Asparagus
2 tablespoons Olive Oil, divided
2 tablespoons Rosemary Leaves, roughly chopped
2 teaspoon Garlic Powder
½ teaspoon Black Pepper
¼ - ½ teaspoon Red Pepper Flakes
Pinch of Kosher Salt

Preparation:

1. Switch the air fryer to 200°C.
2. Spray oil on the potatoes and season with salt and pepper. Air fry for 15-20 minutes until tender. Shake halfway through the cooking time.
3. In a bowl toss asparagus and rosemary in oil and season with garlic powder, salt, pepper and red chili flakes.
4. Add roasted potatoes and asparagus and toss them together.
5. Pop it again in the air fryer for 6-8 minutes until asparagus is crisp.
6. Dish out and serve.

Serving Suggestions: Serve with yoghurt dip.
Variation Tip: You can serve with Grated Parmesan and Fresh Lemon Wedges.
Per Serving: Calories: 444 | Fat: 8g | Sat Fat: 1.3g | Carbohydrates: 82.1g | Fiber: 17.7g | Sugar: 1.4g | Protein: 17.6g

Cheese Eggplant Rolls

Prep: 10 minutes **Cook:** 10 minutes **Serves:** 10

Ingredients:

1 large eggplant
Salt and pepper for seasoning
2 tablespoons cold pressed coconut oil
1 tablespoon pomegranate seeds
1 tablespoon hummus
1 tablespoon lemon juice
¼ tsp of oregano
5 oz. ricotta cheese, crumbled
5 oz. grated cheddar cheese
1 tablespoon chopped basil leaves

Preparation:

1. Switch the air-fryer to 95°C and preheat for 10 minutes.
2. Cut eggplant in thin slices lengthwise.
3. Brush oil on the eggplant slices and Chargrill on a grill pan for 30 seconds each side.
4. Season with salt and pepper.
5. Mix hummus and lemon juice. Spread on one side of each eggplant slice and add ricotta cheese and chopped basil leaves.
6. Roll tightly and place in a heat proof dish.
7. Garnish with grated cheddar cheese and sprinkle oregano.
8. Switch the air fryer at 95°C and place the dish in the air fryer.
9. Air fry for 10 minutes until the cheese melts.
10. Serve warm and garnish with pomegranate seeds.

Serving Suggestions: Serve with your favorite greens
Variation Tip: You can add cayenne pepper.
Per Serving: Calories: 318| Fat: 22.1g|Sat Fat: 15.3g|Carbohydrates: 15.7g|Fiber: 4.6g|Sugar: 6.8g|Protein: 14.6g

Pesto Egg and Cherry Tomato Muffins

⏰ **Prep: 10 minutes** 🍳 **Cook: 20 minutes** 📚 **Serves: 12**

Ingredients:

Cooking oil for spray
18 cherry tomatoes, quartered
3 oz. feta cheese, crumbled
6 medium eggs, lightly beaten
30ml milk
2 tablespoons pesto

Preparation:

1. Switch the air-fryer to 200°C and begin preheating.
2. Spray oil to the muffin tin.
3. In a bowl whisk eggs with milk and pesto.
4. Line tomatoes in the muffin tin, add egg mixture and top with feta cheese.
5. Air fry for 20 minutes until the mixture is firm.
6. Remove from air fryer and let it cool for 2 minutes.
7. Serve warm.

Serving Suggestions: Serve with cream cheese.
Variation Tip: You can add your favorite seasoning for taste variations.
Per Serving: Calories: 74 | Fat: 5g | Sat Fat: 2g | Carbohydrates: 1g | Fiber: 0g | Sugar: 0g | Protein: 5g.

Chocolate and Pear Flapjacks

⏰ **Prep: 10 minutes** 🍳 **Cook: 15 minutes** 📚 **Serves: 4**

Ingredients:

11 oz. porridge oats
4 tablespoon honey
5 oz. butter, plus a little extra for the tin
5 oz. light brown soft sugar
4 oz. dark chocolate, melted
4 pear halves drained from a can

Preparation:

1. Switch the air fryer at 175°C and preheat for 10 minutes.
2. Grease a pan that fits in the air fryer.
3. In a saucepan melt butter, brown sugar and honey. Once melted take it off from the heat. 4. Dice pears into small chunks.
5. Fold out and pears in the butter mixture. Mix well to combine.
6. Add the mixture in the greased pan and press with the back of the spoon.
7. Place in the microwave and cook for 10 minutes.
8. Prepare topping: Microwave chocolate for 20 seconds, stir and then microwave again for 15 seconds.
9. Once the flapjacks are done remove them from the air fryer. Cut squares and drizzle melted chocolate once flapjacks are cooled down.
10. Serve.

Serving Suggestions: Serve with tea.
Variation Tip: You can use hazelnuts or pecans as well.
Per Serving: Calories: 320 | Fat: 16g | Sat Fat: 9g | Carbohydrates: 39g | Fiber: 3g | Sugar: 0g | Protein: 4g

| Chapter 2 Snack and Appetizer Recipes

Cheesy Hash Brown Casserole

⏱ **Prep: 10 minutes**   🍲 **Cook: 10 minutes**   ◈ **Serves: 2**

Ingredients:

2 eggs
1 large potato, coarsely grated
1 tablespoon plain flour
3 spring onions, finely sliced
4 tablespoons cheddar, grated
1 tablespoon vegetable oil

Preparation:

1. Switch the air fryer to 175°C.
2. Drain all the water from the potatoes.
3. Whisk eggs and add potatoes, flour, cheese and sliced spring onions. season generously with salt and pepper.
4. Grease a small heat proof dish with oil and add potato mixture. Cook in the air fryer for 7 minutes.
5. Spread remaining grated cheese on the top and cook for another 3-4 minutes or until the cheese has been melted.
6. Serve Warm.

Serving Suggestions: Serve by garnishing dried parsley or chili flakes.
Variation Tip: You can also use sausage meat for taste variation.
Per Serving: Calories: 661 | Fat: 35g | Sat Fat: 12g | Carbohydrates: 54g | Fiber: 5g | Sugar: 0g | Protein: 30g

Mini Cheese Chorizo Frittatas

⏱ **Prep: 8 minutes**   🍲 **Cook: 20 minutes**   ◈ **Serves: 8**

Ingredients:

5 oz. potatoes
6 eggs, beaten
4 oz. chorizo diced
Salt and pepper for seasoning
3 oz. frozen peas, defrosted
few sprigs of parsley, finely chopped
2 oz. cheddar, grated

Preparation:

1. Boil potatoes for 10- 15 minutes. once cooked, drain and set them aside.
2. Cut the potatoes into slices.
3. Switch the air fryer to 200°C and preheat for 10 minutes.
4. Line a muffin tray that fits in the air fryer with muffin liners.
5. In a bowl add eggs, peas, parsley and chorizo. Season with salt and pepper.
6. Line the muffin tray with potato slices and spoon out the egg mixture. Top with cheese and place the muffin tray in the air fryer. Cook for 15-20 minutes until frittatas are firm and lightly browned.
7. Serve warm.

Serving Suggestions: You can serve it with sweet Thai chili sauce.
Variation Tip: You can serve it with tartar sauce too.
Per Serving: Calories: 172 | Fat: 11g | Sat Fat: 4g | Carbohydrates: 5g | Fiber: 1g | Sugar: 0g | Protein: 12g

Lemon Cream Scones

⏰ **Prep: 10 minutes**   🍲 **Cook: 12 minutes**   ≋ **Serves: 10**

Ingredients:

2¾ self-raising flour, plus extra for dusting
1 tablespoon baking powder
½ cup lemonade
¼ cup caster sugar
½ cup double cream
1 egg, beaten

Preparation:

1. Switch the air-fryer at 200°C and preheat for 10 minutes.
2. Mix sugar, flour and baking powder in a bowl.
3. Pour cream and lemonade in the flour mixture and knead to a soft dough.
4. Roll the dough to 2cm-thickness and cut circles with the cookie cutter.
5. Brush the top of the scones with beaten egg and place scones in the air fryer for 12 minutes. Cook the rest in batches.
6. Serve with tea.

Serving Suggestions: Serve with butter and marmalade
Variation Tip: You can add butter instead of double cream.
Per Serving: Calories: 217 | Fat: 7g | Sat Fat: 4g | Carbohydrates: 33g | Fiber: 1g | Sugar: 4g | Protein: 17g

Mini Crumpets Pizza

⏰ **Prep: 20 minutes**   🍲 **Cook: 5 minutes**   ≋ **Serves: 6**

Ingredients:

6 crumpets
4 tablespoons passata
4 tablespoons ketchup
½ teaspoon dried oregano
peppers, cherry tomatoes, red onion, olives, ham and basil- chopped in small pieces for the topping
3 oz. cheddar cheese, grated

Preparation:

1. Switch the air fryer at 175°C and lightly toast the crumpets.
2. Mix passata, ketchup and oregano together.
3. Spread sauce over the crumpets, followed by chopped vegetables and top with grated cheese.
4. Place the crumpets in the air fryer tray and cook for 3-4 minutes until the cheese has melted and turned golden.
5. Dish out and serve right away.

Serving Suggestions: Serve with ketchup and garnish with chopped parsley
Variation Tip: You can also use pepperoni slices.
Per Serving: Calories: 145 | Fat: 5g | Sat Fat: 3g | Carbohydrates: 18g | Fiber: 1g | Sugar: 2g | Protein: 6g

Chapter 2 Snack and Appetizer Recipes

Mini Bean and Sausage Pies with Cheese

⏲ Prep: 25 minutes 🍲 Cook: 20 minutes 🍽 Serves: 4

Ingredients:

4 sausages, cooked, then sliced into rounds
14 oz. can chopped haricot beans, drained and rinsed
4 spring onions, chopped
5 oz. passata
Pinch of dried oregano
Salt and pepper for seasoning
11 oz. ready-rolled puff pastry sheet
Pinch of sugar
2 oz. cheddar, grated
1 egg, beaten

Preparation:

1. Switch the air-fryer for 20 minutes at 200°C.
2. Prepare filling: Combine sausages, beans, passata, spring onions, cheese, oregano and sugar. Season with salt and pepper. Reserve some cheese for the topping.
3. Roll the pastry until 1cm-thick. Cut rectangles and add filling and wrap by folding the other half. Cut slits on top and brush with beaten egg. Sprinkle the reserved cheese on top.
4. Cook for 20 minutes until its golden brown.
5. Serve warm.

Serving Suggestions: Serve with salad and ketchup
Variation Tip: You can add your favorite seasoning to the filling.
Per Serving: Calories: 570 | Fat: 36g | Sat Fat: 16g | Carbohydrates: 38g | Fiber: 8g | Sugar: 4g | Protein: 20g

Cheesy Apple and Potato Pasties

⏲ Prep: 30 minutes 🍲 Cook: 25 minutes 🍽 Serves: 6

Ingredients:

11 oz. cold butter
4 cups all-purpose flour, plus extra for dusting
¼ cup caster sugar (optional)
Salt and pepper for seasoning
2 medium potatoes, boiled and cubed
3 Granny Smith apples, peeled and cubed
12 oz. hard cheese, grated
Milk for brushing the pasties

Preparation:

1. Switch the air fryer at 175°C and preheat for 10 minutes.
2. Mix flour, salt, pepper and butter to form a crumbly texture. Add some cold water to form a firm dough. Cover and let it rest for 20 minutes.
3. For the Filling: Mix potatoes, cheese, apples, sugar and season with salt and pepper.
4. Make six balls out of the dough and roll out. Place in the pastry dough, add a tablespoon of filling and close the mold to shape the pasty.
5. Brush milk on the pasties and place in the air fryer.
6. Cook for 25 minutes and remove once they are golden brown in color.
7. Repeat the same steps for the remaining batches.

Serving Suggestions: Serve with cream cheese.
Variation Tip: You can use Lincolnshire Poacher or Cornish cheddar work well too.
Per Serving: Calories: 188 | Fat: 14g | Sat Fat: 3g | Carbohydrates: 10g | Fiber: 1g | Sugar: 1g | Protein: 7g

Chapter 2 Snack and Appetizer Recipes

Golden Prawn Balls

⏰ **Prep:** 45 minutes   🍲 **Cook:** 6 minutes   🍽 **Serves:** 6

Ingredients:

- 9 oz. thawed prawn meat, cleaned and deveined
- 1 teaspoon olive oil, plus extra, to brush
- 1 green shallot, very thinly sliced
- 1 teaspoon ginger, finely grated
- 2 garlic cloves, finely chopped
- 1 egg white
- ½ teaspoon caster sugar
- 2 teaspoon soy sauce
- 5oz sesame seeds, lightly toasted
- 2 eggs, lightly whisked
- Bread crumbs for coating

Preparation:

1. Switch the air-fryer to 75°C and preheat for 10 minutes.
2. In a food processor add prawns, sugar, garlic, ginger, soya sauce, sugar, egg white, oil and sesame seeds. Process until a paste like consistency forms. Fold chopped shallots and place the mixture in the fridge for 30 minutes.
3. In two separate bowls, place eggs and bread crumbs. Take one tablespoon of the mixture and roll into a ball. Dunk in egg and coat breadcrumbs.
4. Air fry for 6 minutes or until golden. Cook the remaining prawn balls in the same manner.
5. Serve warm and enjoy.

Serving Suggestions: Serve with honey mustard sauce
Variation Tip: You can spice it up by using cayenne pepper.
Per Serving: Calories: 198 | Fat: 14g | Sat Fat: 2.2g | Carbohydrates: 7g | Fiber: 2.9g | Sugar: 0.6g | Protein: 12.8g

Puff Pastry Pigs in a Blanket

⏰ **Prep:** 10 minutes   🍲 **Cook:** 25 minutes   🍽 **Serves:** 8

Ingredients:

- ½ sheet of 11 oz. ready-rolled puff pastry
- 16 pork chipolatas
- ½ tablespoon vegetable oil, for greasing
- 1 egg yolk, beaten, to glaze

Preparation:

1. Switch the air-fryer to 80°C and preheat for 5 minutes.
2. Grease the air fryer sheet pan with oil.
3. Cut 16 strips from the puff pastry. Each should be 10 cm-long.
4. Wrap around chipolatas and place in the fridge for 15 minutes.
5. Once chilled, brush them with beaten egg yolk and air fry for 25 minutes.
6. Cook until the pastry is puffed and golden brown remove from the air fryer. Cook other batches in the same manner.
7. Serve and Enjoy!

Serving Suggestions: Serve with your favorite dip.
Variation Tip: You can garnish with sesame seeds as well.
Per Serving: Calories: 205 | Fat: 15g | Sat Fat: 6g | Carbohydrates: 9g | Fiber: 1g | Sugar: 1g | Protein: 8g

Chapter 2 Snack and Appetizer Recipes

Crispy Honey Mustard Halloumi Bars

⏰ Prep: 20 minutes   🍲 Cook: 10 minutes   ❄ Serves: 8

Ingredients:

1 lb. haloumi cut in 1cm wide batons
2 teaspoons Mustard Powder
¼ cup plain flour
1 egg, lightly whisked
1 cup panko breadcrumbs

Honey Mustard Mayo
½ cup mayonnaise
¼ cup thickened cream
1 tablespoon honey
2 teaspoons Mustard Powder

Preparation:

1. Switch the air-fryer to 200°C and preheat for 10 minutes.
2. Prepare sauce: Combine all the honey mustard sauce ingredients and mix well.
3. Prepare coating by combining flour and mustard powder.
4. Lightly whisk egg in a separate bowl and keep panko bread crumbs in a shallow container.
5. Coat haloumi in flour mixture, then dunk in egg and finally coat bread crumbs.
6. Air fry haloumi for 10 minutes until crisped and golden.
7. Cook the other batch in the same manner. 8. Dish out and serve.

Serving Suggestions: Serve with your favorite dipping sauce.
Variation Tip: You can also use your favorite seasoning mix in the flour mixture.
Per Serving: Calories: 213 | Fat: 17g | Sat Fat: 6g | Carbohydrates: 5g | Fiber: 1g | Sugar: 1g | Protein: 9g

Cinnamon Apple Crisps

⏰ Prep: 5 minutes   🍲 Cook: 30 minutes   ❄ Serves: 4

Ingredients:

2 Granny Smiths   cinnamon, for sprinkling

Preparation:

1. Switch the air-fryer at 175°C.
2. Core and slice apples through the equator into very thin slices.
3. Line the apples in a single layer and cook for 30 minutes until crisp and golden.
4. Cook all the batches in the same way and remove in a large bowl.
5. Sprinkle cinnamon and toss carefully.

Serving Suggestions: Serve topped with lemon wedges.
Variation Tip: You can skip nutmeg for taste variation.
Per Serving: Calories: 90 | Fat: 0.3g | Sat Fat: 0g | Carbohydrates: 22g | Fiber: 3.3g | Sugar: 22g | Protein: 0.8g

Chapter 2 Snack and Appetizer Recipes | 23

Sticky Beef Bites

🕐 Prep: 15 minutes 🍳 Cook: 40 minutes 🍽 Serves: 8

Ingredients:

2.2 lbs. boneless beef
1 tablespoon brown sugar
3 teaspoons smoked paprika
2 teaspoons plain flour
1 teaspoon onion powder
½ teaspoon garlic powder
Olive oil spray
Sticky Golden Syrup Sauce
¼ cup butter
2 tablespoons golden syrup
2 tablespoons barbecue sauce
1 tablespoon bourbon
2 teaspoon sriracha sauce

Preparation:

1. Prepare coating: Combine paprika, sugar, flour, garlic powder and onion powder in a bowl.
2. Toss boneless beef pieces with the coating and place in the fridge for 2 hours.
3. Switch the air fryer to 200°C.
4. Spray beef with oil and season well. Place beef cubes in the air fryer and cook for 40 minutes. Shake the basket halfway through cooking. Once browned transfer to a bowl. Cook the remaining beef in the same way.
5. For the sticky sauce: Heat butter, barbecue sauce, golden syrup, bourbon and sriracha in a small saucepan. Season with salt and pepper. Cook for 3 minutes or until you get a thick, smooth mixture.
6. Drizzle sauce on the beef. Insert skewers in the sticky beef bites.
7. Serve and enjoy.

Serving Suggestions: Serve with parsley
Variation Tip: You can garnish parmesan cheese as well.
Per Serving: Calories: 998 | Fat: 99g | Sat Fat: 37.4g | Carbohydrates: 8g | Fiber: 0.4g | Sugar: 3.7g | Protein: 16.8g

Parmesan Carrot Fries

🕐 Prep: 10 minutes 🍳 Cook: 20 minutes 🍽 Serves: 2

Ingredients:

3-4 carrots
1 tablespoon olive oil
1 clove garlic, crushed
2 tablespoons Grated Parmesan
1 pinch salt and freshly cracked black pepper, optional
1 teaspoon fresh parsley, chopped

Preparation:

1. Add crushed garlic to the olive oil and stir well.
2. Cut the carrots in the form of fries and toss olive oil and garlic mixture.
3. Mix the parmesan with salt and black pepper.
4. Toss carrots in the parmesan mixture.
5. Add carrot fries on an air fryer basket in an even layer.
6. Air fry at 175°C for 16-20 minutes. Shake halfway through for crispier carrot fries.
7. Top with freshly chopped parsley.
8. Serve warm and enjoy.

Serving Suggestions: Serve with garlic mayo dip.
Variation Tip: You can top it up with crushed red peppers.
Per Serving: Calories: 202| Fat: 13g | Sat Fat: 5g| Carbohydrates: 13.5g|Fiber: 3g|Sugar: 6g|Protein: 10g

Grilled Zucchini Cheese Rolls

⏱ **Prep: 15 minutes** 🍲 **Cook: 5 minutes** ≋ **Serves: 8**

Ingredients:

2 medium zucchini, thinly sliced lengthways
3 oz. soft goat's cheese
3 teaspoon milk
Salt and pepper for seasoning
1 tablespoon finely chopped fresh mint leaves
Olive oil cooking spray

Preparation:

1. Spray a grill pan with oil. Chargrill zucchini slices for 1-2 minutes, each side. Transfer onto a plate and set aside to cool.
2. For the filling: Combine mint, cheese, and milk in a small bowl. Season with salt and pepper according to your taste.
3. Spread cheese mixture on one side of each zucchini slice.
4. Roll up tightly and Secure with a toothpick.
5. Switch the air-fryer to 175°C and place zucchini cheese rolls in the air fryer basket for 3 minutes.
6. Dish out and serve.

Serving Suggestions: Garnish it with chopped mint.
Variation Tip: You can use cream instead of milk for the variation in taste.
Per Serving: Calories: 75 | Fat: 4.8g | Sat Fat: 3.2g | Carbohydrates: 3.8g | Fiber: 1.2g | Sugar: 2.1g | Protein: 5.3g

Chapter 3 Vegetable and Sides Recipes

Roasted Cheese Garlic Dip

Prep: 10 minutes Cook: 40 minutes Serves: 6

Ingredients:

4 large heads of garlic
6 tablespoons olive oil
2 sprigs of fresh thyme
9-10oz soft goat's cheese
1 tablespoon of lemon juice
Dash of milk if necessary
2 tablespoons chopped fresh herbs - a mixture of parsley, tarragon, and chives.
Salt and pepper for seasoning

Preparation:

1. Switch the air fryer to 200°C.
2. Slice off the heads of the garlic.
3. Place garlic, oil, and sprigs of thyme to a heat-proof dish and seal with foil.
4. Cook garlic in the air fryer for 40 minutes.
5. Once cooked, garlic should be soft and mushy.
6. In a bowl, beat the cheese until creamy. Squeeze out the garlic from its skin and add in the cheese. Blend well with a dash of milk.
7. Beat in the herbs and squeeze lemon juice. Season with pepper and salt.
8. Dish out and serve with the vegetable platter.

Serving Suggestions: Serve with pomegranate seeds on top.
Variation Tip: You can use ricotta or Philadelphia cheese as well.
Per Serving: Calories: 430 | Fat: 26g | Sat Fat: 2g | Carbohydrates: 38g | Fiber: 0g | Sugar: 9g | Protein: 14g

Chili Parsnip and Cauliflower Soup

Prep: 10 minutes Cook: 30 minutes Serves: 4

Ingredients:

1 tablespoon olive oil
2 oz. of butter
11 oz. cauliflower florets
7 oz. parsnips, chopped
4 cups vegetable stock
1 tablespoon fennel seed
3 green chilies, deseeded and chopped
2 onions, chopped
3 garlic cloves, sliced
1 teaspoon grated ginger
1 tablespoon lemon juice
½ teaspoon lemon zest
1 tablespoon chives, chopped
Salt and pepper for seasoning

Preparation:

1. Switch the air fryer to 200°C. preheat for 5 minutes.
2. Add parsnips and cauliflower florets to a heat-proof dish. Drizzle oil and season with salt and pepper. Add one cup of vegetable stock to the dish as well.
3. Cook vegetables in the air fryer for 20 minutes until they are soft.
4. In a pan, heat butter and sauté onion along with ginger and garlic.
5. Transfer cooked vegetables to the pan along with fennel seeds, chopped chilies, lemon juice and lemon zest.
6. Add the remaining vegetable stock and bring it to a boil. Once boiled, let it simmer for 10 minutes.
7. Blend with the stick blender until it is smooth in consistency.
8. Ladle out in the bowls, sprinkle with chives and serve.

Serving Suggestions: Serve with crusted bread.
Variation Tip: You can drizzle melted butter and chili flakes.
Per Serving: Calories: 133 | Fat: 4g | Sat Fat: 1g | Carbohydrates: 18g | Fiber: 9g | Sugar: 11g | Protein: 7g

Cream and Cheese Stuffed Pumpkin

⏰ **Prep: 10 minutes** 🍲 **Cook: 40 minutes** 🍽 **Serves: 6**

Ingredients:

1 lb. pumpkin (that can fit in the air fryer basket)
⅔ cup milk
10 fl oz. double cream
3 garlic cloves, crushed
3 ounces of grated parmesan
2 teaspoons thyme leaves
A pinch of black pepper

Preparation:

1. Switch the air fryer to 175°C and preheat for 10 minutes.
2. Wash the pumpkin and slice off the head. Scoop out the strands and seeds.
3. Place the pumpkin in the air fryer tray.
4. In a saucepan, heat milk, cream, thyme, and garlic till they start bubbling.
5. Pour the cream mixture into the pumpkin and add half of the parmesan.
6. Put the head back on the pumpkin.
7. Air fry pumpkin for 30 minutes.
8. Sprinkle black pepper and remaining parmesan cheese and air fry for another 10 minutes until the cheese turns golden.
9. Serve with toasted bread slices.

Serving Suggestions: Garnish with basil leaves, parsley, and chili flakes.
Variation Tip: You can also garnish it with roasted pancetta for taste variation.
Per Serving: Calories: 342 | Fat: 32g | Sat Fat: 18g | Carbohydrates: 6g | Fiber: 2g | Sugar: 5g | Protein: 8g

Tomatoes-Stuffed Peppers with Cheese

⏰ **Prep: 15 minutes** 🍲 **Cook: 20 minutes** 🍽 **Serves: 4**

Ingredients:

2 large peppers, halved, deseeded but stalks left on
7 oz. chopped tomatoes
1 red onion, halved and sliced
1 garlic clove, finely grated
Salt and pepper
1 red chili, deseeded and finely chopped
1 small aubergine cut into small cubes
1 large egg
1 teaspoon pumpkin spice mix
4 oz. low-fat feta cheese, crumbled
5oz low-fat fromage frais

Preparation:

1. Switch the air-fryer to 85°C.
2. Place peppers, skin-side up, in the air fryer and roast for 10 minutes. Once done, remove from the air fryer and set aside.
3. For the filling: Add tomatoes, onions, garlic, and aubergine in a pan and cook for 10 minutes. Season with salt and pepper.
4. In a bowl beat egg, formage frais and feta.
5. In a dish, place peppers and fill with the vegetable mixture generously.
6. Press down from the back of the spoon and fill as much as you can. Top it up with feta mixture and sprinkle pumpkin spice.
7. Cook stuffed peppers in the air fryer for 10 minutes until the topping is firm. 8. Serve warm.

Serving Suggestions: Serve with a green salad and lime wedges
Variation Tip: Add in some cayenne pepper for taste enhancement.
Per Serving: Calories: 288 | Fat: 7g | Sat Fat: 3g | Carbohydrates: 39g | Fiber: 15g | Sugar: 26g | Protein: 19g

Easy British Mackerel Fillets

⏱ **Prep: 5 minutes**　🍴 **Cook: 12 minutes**　📚 **Serves: 2**

Ingredients:

1 tablespoon rapeseed oil
2 mackerel fillets, skin on
Salt and black pepper, to taste

Preparation:

1. Switch the temperature of the Air fryer to 200°C.
2. In a small bowl, dust the mackerel fillets with salt and pepper, then scrub rapeseed with oil.
3. Layer the mackerel fillets into the Air fryer basket and then air fry for 12 minutes, flipping once in between.
4. Dish out and serve warm.

Serving Suggestions: Serve with peri peri sauce.
Variation Tip: You can use your favorite spices, herbs, and seasonings.
Per Serving: Calories: 298 | Fat: 22.7g | Sat Fat: 4.2g | Carbohydrates: 0g | Fiber: 0g | Sugar: 0g | Protein: 21g

Roasted Vegetables with Herbs

⏱ **Prep: 10 minutes**　🍴 **Cook: 20 minutes**　📚 **Serves: 4**

Ingredients:

3 tablespoons olive oil
1 aubergine, cut into chunks
2 carrots, cut in lengthwise
2 parsnips, cut in lengthwise
1 red onion, cut into wedges
2 courgettes, cut into chunks
4 garlic cloves smashed
3 sprigs of thyme
7 oz. cherry tomatoes
A handful of basil leaves
Zest of 1 lemon
Lemon Juice 2 tablespoons
Salt and pepper

Preparation:

1. Switch the air fryer to 150°C. Preheat for 10 minutes.
2. Place vegetables in a heat-proof platter that fits in the air fryer.
3. Mix garlic, oil, lemon zest, lemon juice, basil leaves, salt, and pepper in the vegetables.
4. Cook the vegetables in the air fryer for 20 minutes.
5. Serve them as a side dish once cooked and crisped.

Serving Suggestions: You can serve it with hummus
Variation Tip: you can add a variety of your favorite vegetables.
Per Serving: Calories: 198 | Fat: 12g | Sat Fat: 3g | Carbohydrates: 12g | Fiber: 7g | Sugar: 11g | Protein: 6g

Chapter 3 Vegetable and Sides Recipes

Cheese Vegetable Pie

⏲ Prep: 15 minutes 🍳 Cook: 40 minutes 🍽 Serves: 4

Ingredients:

4 tablespoons butter
11 oz. ready-to-cook, shortcrust pastry
2½ cups milk
Salt and pepper
1 cup broccoli florets
1 cup frozen peas
2 teaspoons mustard powder
¾ cup grated cheddar cheese
2 large potatoes, cut into small chunks.
1 cup cauliflower florets
¼ cup flour
1 egg lightly beaten

Preparation:

1. Prepare sauce: Melt butter and stir mustard and flour. Add milk gradually. Cook it until the sauce is thick and creamy. Fold in cheese until it is melted.
2. Switch the air fryer to 150°C and preheat for 10 minutes.
3. In a large pan, boil potatoes, broccoli, peas, and cauliflower one by one. Drain and pat dry.
4. Dump boiled vegetables in a mixing bowl and add creamy sauce. Fold the sauce carefully. Season with salt and pepper.
5. Roll pie crust until ¼inches thick.
6. Add vegetables to a deep dish and cover it with the pie crust. Make 3-4 slits on the crust and brush with the egg.
7. Place the pie dish in the air fryer and cook for 40 minutes until it is golden brown. 8. Serve and enjoy.

Serving Suggestions: Sprinkle some seasoning over the pie and serve.
Variation Tip: You can use a variety of other vegetables for the dish.
Per Serving: Calories: 604 | Fat: 34g | Sat Fat: 19g | Carbohydrates: 45g | Fiber: 9g | Sugar: 14g | Protein: 33g

Roasted Vegetables and Stilton Soup

⏲ Prep: 10 minutes 🍳 Cook: 15 minutes 🍽 Serves: 4

Ingredients:

2 tablespoons rapeseed oil
1 onion, finely chopped
1 stick celery, sliced
Salt and pepper for seasoning
1 leek, sliced
1 medium potato, diced
2 tablespoons of butter
4 cups vegetable stock
1 lb. broccoli, roughly chopped
5 oz. stilton, or other blue cheese, crumbled

Preparation:

1. Switch the air fryer to 40°C and preheat for 5 minutes.
2. Spray broccoli with oil and cook in the air fryer for 5 minutes.
3. In a pan, add butter and sauté onion till translucent. Add celery, leeks, and potatoes along with the vegetable stock. Bring it to a boil and simmer till the potatoes are soft.
4. Then add broccoli and let it simmer for 10 minutes.
5. Blend with the stick blender and add crumbled stilton. Season with salt and pepper.
6. Ladle out in bowls and Serve warm.

Serving Suggestions: You can garnish with croutons.
Variation Tip: You can use any other crumbled blue cheese.
Per Serving: Calories: 340 | Fat: 21g | Sat Fat: 9.6g | Carbohydrates: 13.8 | Fiber: 6.9g | Sugar: 5g | Protein: 24.3g

Crispy Spicy Oysters

⏰ **Prep:** 15 minutes   🍲 **Cook:** 12 minutes   🍽 **Serves:** 4

Ingredients:

- ½ cup flour
- 2 cans oysters, 8 oz. each
- 1 teaspoon Cajun seasoning
- ½ teaspoon black pepper
- 3 tablespoons hot sauce
- 1 teaspoon salt
- 2 eggs
- 2 cups Panko bread crumbs

Preparation:

1. Switch the temperature of the Air fryer to 175°C.
2. In a small bowl, place panko.
3. In another bowl, whisk egg with hot sauce and in a third bowl, merge flour, Cajun seasoning, salt, and pepper.
4. Dip the oysters in the egg mixture after dredging them in the flour mixture.
5. Coat with the panko and layer the oysters into the Air fryer basket.
6. Cook for 12 minutes, flipping once in between.
7. Dish out and serve warm.

Serving Suggestions: You can serve it with coleslaw.
Variation Tip: You can also use Old Bay seasoning.
Per Serving: Calories: 337 | Fat: 6.3g | Sat Fat: 1.6g | Carbohydrates: 54.2g | Fiber: 3.4g | Sugar: 4.4g | Protein: 15.1g

Green Asparagus Soup

⏰ **Prep:** 10 minutes   🍲 **Cook:** 20 minutes   🍽 **Serves:** 4

Ingredients:

- 12 oz. asparagus spear, stalks chopped
- 2 large handfuls spinach
- 2 tablespoons butter
- 3 shallots, finely sliced
- vegetable oil for spraying
- 2 garlic cloves, crushed
- 3 cups vegetable stock
- Salt and pepper for seasoning

Preparation:

1. Switch the air-fryer to 175°C and preheat for 10 minutes.
2. Spray oil on the asparagus stalks and season with salt and pepper.
3. Cook asparagus in the air fryer for 10 minutes.
4. In a pan, heat butter and add garlic and chopped shallots. Sauté for a minute, then add spinach, cooked asparagus, and stock. Let it simmer for 10 minutes.
5. Blend with the stick blender and check for seasoning.
6. Serve piping hot as a side dish, and enjoy.

Serving Suggestions: serve with rustic bread (preferably sourdough)
Variation Tip: You can also top it with salted pumpkin seeds, asparagus tips, and croutons.
Per Serving: Calories: 101 | Fat: 8g | Sat Fat: 4g | Carbohydrates: 4g | Fiber: 4g | Sugar: 4g | Protein: 4g

Chapter 3 Vegetable and Sides Recipes

Rosemary Vegetable Soup

⏲ Prep: 10 minutes 🍲 Cook: 40 minutes 🍽 Serves: 2

Ingredients:

1½ cups chopped vegetables such as onions, celery, and carrots
2 cups potatoes, cubed
2 tablespoons butter
1 onion chopped
1 sprig of rosemary
1 tablespoon oil
2 cloves of garlic, smashed
4 cups chicken stock
Salt and pepper
2 tablespoons crème fraîche
1 teaspoon chopped parsley to serve

Preparation:

1. Switch the air-fryer to 200°C and preheat for 10 minutes.
2. Drizzle oil on the vegetables and coat well. Place vegetables in the dish and air fry them for about 20 minutes.
3. Remove the vegetable once they are soft.
4. In a saucepan, add butter and sauté onions until translucent. Add garlic, roasted vegetables, and rosemary along with the stock.
5. Let it simmer for 20 minutes. Once the flavors are mingled well, discard the rosemary sprig and blend everything with the stick blender.
6. You should get a smooth consistency. Check the seasoning and add according to your liking.
7. Ladle out in the soup bowls and garnish with crème fraîche and chopped parsley

Serving Suggestions: Serve with crusted bread
Variation Tip: You can add crumbled blue cheese as well.
Per Serving: Calories: 218 | Fat: 7g | Sat Fat: 6g | Carbohydrates: 32g | Fiber: 6g | Sugar: 7g | Protein: 4g

Creamy Cauliflower Potato Soup

⏲ Prep: 10 minutes 🍲 Cook: 2 minutes 🍽 Serves: 6

Ingredients:

1 lb. cauliflower florets
1 medium potato, cut into chunks
¼ cup unsalted butter
1 onion, roughly chopped
2 cups whole milk
4 cups vegetable stock
¼ cup double cream
Chopped parsley to serve
Salt and pepper for seasoning
Extra virgin olive oil for drizzling

Preparation:

1. Switch the air-fryer to 200°C and preheat for 10 minutes.
2. Spray potatoes and cauliflower with oil. Add salt and pepper.
3. Place them in the air-fryer dish and cook for about 15 minutes. Shake them halfway through.
4. Once crisp and golden brown, remove from the air-fryer.
5. In a saucepan, melt butter and cook onions until translucent. Add cooked cauliflowers and potatoes with the stock and milk and cook for 10 minutes.
6. Once the vegetables are soft, blend the soup until smooth.
7. Check the seasoning, and you can add salt and pepper as per your liking. Stir double cream and heat the soup again.
8. Garnish with parsley and drizzle olive oil.

Serving Suggestions: Serve with crusted bread
Variation Tip: You can sprinkle cayenne pepper for variation in taste.
Per Serving: Calories: 317 | Fat: 23g | Sat Fat: 14g | Carbohydrates: 18g | Fiber: 4g | Sugar: 11g | Protein: 8g

Cream Carrot Soup with Pancetta Bread

⏲ **Prep: 15 minutes**   🍲 **Cook: 45 minutes**   ❖ **Serves: 2**

Ingredients:

- 25 oz. carrot, cut into cubes
- 3 cups vegetable stock
- 4 garlic cloves with skin
- A few thyme sprigs, plus an extra to garnish
- 2 tablespoons of butter
- 2 onions, finely chopped
- 6 tablespoons double cream
- 2 tablespoons olive oil
- Salt and pepper.
- 6 slices pancetta
- 2 thick slices of rustic bread

Preparation:

1. Switch the air-fryer to 200°C and preheat for 10 minutes.
2. Toss carrots with oil, garlic, and rosemary sprigs and air fry for 20 minutes.
3. In a saucepan, heat butter and sauté onions. Dump in the roasted carrots, discard sprigs of thyme, and pour vegetable stock.
4. Let it simmer for 20 minutes and season with salt and pepper.
5. Blend it with a stick blender to get a smooth consistency.
6. Add 5 tablespoons of cream and mix well. Adjust seasoning as needed.
7. Air fry pancetta and bread slices at 95°C for 5 minutes until crisp.
8. Ladle out soup in the serving bowl and garnish cream over it.
9. Serve with bread and crisped pancetta.

Serving Suggestions: Serve topped with cilantro.

Variation Tip: You can also use chicken or beef stock instead of vegetable stock.

Per Serving: Calories: 828 | Fat: 57g | Sat Fat: 26g | Carbohydrates: 51g | Fiber: 12g | Sugar: 34g | Protein: 28g

Chapter 4 Fish and Seafood Recipes

Fried Oysters with Cheesy Garlic Butter

⏰ **Prep: 10 minutes** 🍲 **Cook: 7 minutes** 🍽 **Serves: 4**

Ingredients:

½ stick butter, melted
8 oysters on the half shell
2 tablespoons lemon juice
2 garlic cloves, grated
1 teaspoon Worcestershire sauce
¼ cup parmigiano reggiano, grated
1 tablespoon fresh parsley, chopped
Salt, cayenne, and black pepper, to taste

Preparation:

1. Switch the temperature of the Air fryer to 175°C.
2. In a large bowl, merge butter, garlic, Worcestershire sauce, parsley, lemon juice, salt, cayenne, and pepper.
3. Layer oysters in the Air fryer basket and then cook for about 2 minutes.
4. Dish out and top each oyster with 1 tablespoon of the butter mixture.
5. Top with cheese and cook for about 5 minutes.
6. Serve hot.

Serving Suggestions: Serve with cocktail sauce or your favorite dipping sauce.
Variation Tip: Serve with bread and hot sauce.
Per Serving: Calories: 215| Fat: 16.1g| Sat Fat: 9.3g| Carbohydrates: 5.5g|Fiber: 0.1g|Sugar: 1.5g|Protein: 11.8g

Air Fryer Herbed Salmon

⏰ **Prep: 5 minutes** 🍲 **Cook: 10 minutes** 🍽 **Serves: 4**

Ingredients:

1 teaspoon salt
1 teaspoon mixed herbs
4 salmon fillets
1 teaspoon black pepper
1 teaspoon garlic granules
½ tablespoon olive oil

Preparation:

1. Switch the temperature of the Air fryer to 180°C.
2. In a bowl, merge the salt, mixed herbs, black pepper, and garlic granules.
3. Rub a little olive oil over each salmon fillet and then coat gently with the seasoning.
4. Layer salmon fillets in the Air fryer basket and then air fry for about 10 minutes.
5. Dish out and serve warm.

Serving Suggestions: Serve with cooked seasonal greens and quinoa.
Variation Tip: You can also use cod instead of salmon.
Per Serving: Calories: 253 | Fat: 12.8g | Sat Fat: 1.8g | Carbohydrates: 0.7g | Fiber: 0.2g | Sugar: 0g | Protein: 34.7g

Marinated Lime Salmon

⏰ **Prep: 10 minutes**　🍲 **Cook: 20 minutes**　🍱 **Serves: 4**

Ingredients:

- 3 tablespoons pure maple syrup
- 1 lime, zested and juiced
- 3 tablespoons soy sauce
- 4 (4 oz.) salmon fillets, skin-on

Preparation:

1. Switch the temperature of the Air fryer to 200°C.
2. In a small bowl, merge the salmon fillets with lime zest and juice, maple syrup, and soy sauce. Marinate for about 2 hours.
3. Layer the salmon, skin side up in Air fryer basket and then air fry for 10 minutes.
4. In a saucepan, simmer leftover marinade for 10 minutes.
5. Dish out the salmon and serve warm with marinade.

Serving Suggestions: Serve over cooked greens.
Variation Tip: You can use coconut aminos instead of soy sauce.
Per Serving: Calories: 201 | Fat: 7.1g | Sat Fat: 1g | Carbohydrates: 12.7g | Fiber: 0.6g | Sugar: 9.4g | Protein: 22.9g

Roasted Cajun Salmon

⏰ **Prep: 10 minutes**　🍲 **Cook: 8 minutes**　🍱 **Serves: 2**

Ingredients:

- 2 (6 ounce) skin-on salmon fillets
- Cooking spray
- 1 teaspoon brown sugar
- 1 tablespoon Cajun seasoning

Preparation:

1. Switch the temperature of the Air fryer to 200°C.
2. In a small bowl, merge the salmon fillets with Cajun seasoning and brown sugar.
3. Grease the sides of salmon with cooking spray. Layer the salmon in the Air fryer basket and then air fry for 8 minutes.
4. Dish out the salmon and serve warm.

Serving Suggestions: You can serve with pickled cucumbers.
Variation Tip: You can use haddock or cod instead of salmon.
Per Serving: Calories: 280 | Fat: 12.3g | Sat Fat: 3g | Carbohydrates: 1.5g | Fiber: 0g | Sugar: 1.5g | Protein: 41.1g

Honey Glazed Salmon

⏰ **Prep:** 10 minutes   🍲 **Cook:** 9 minutes   ❇ **Serves:** 4

Ingredients:

2 tablespoons soy sauce
4 salmon fillets, boneless
3 tablespoons honey
1 teaspoon sesame seeds
1 teaspoon sea salt

Preparation:

1. Switch the temperature of the Air fryer to 190°C.
2. In a small bowl, merge the soy sauce, honey and sea salt.
3. Rub the salmon with half of the glaze.
4. Layer the salmon in the Air fryer basket and then air fry for 7 minutes.
5. Dish out and trickle with the remaining glaze and sesame seeds.
6. Air fry again for 2 minutes and serve.

Serving Suggestions: Serve with baked asparagus.
Variation Tip: Add 1 teaspoon of chili flakes to the honey glaze for increased spiciness.
Per Serving: Calories: 292 | Fat: 11.4g | Sat Fat: 1.6g | Carbohydrates: 13.8g | Fiber: 0.2g | Sugar: 13.1g | Protein: 35.2g

Salmon with Tomato Beans Salad

⏰ **Prep:** 5 minutes   🍲 **Cook:** 7 minutes   ❇ **Serves:** 6

Ingredients:

4 salmon fillets, scaled
12 cherry tomatoes, halved
9 oz. green beans, trimmed and boiled
2 round shallots, finely chopped
Salt and black pepper, to taste
For the Glaze
3 tablespoons wholegrain mustard
9 oz. sugar snap peas, boiled
2 tablespoons white wine vinegar
3 tablespoons honey

Preparation:

1. Switch the temperature of the Air fryer to 200°C.
2. For the glaze: In a small bowl, merge the honey and mustard.
3. Rub the salmon with half of the glaze and put shallot, vinegar, cherry tomatoes, green beans, and peas in the remaining glaze.
4. Layer the salmon in the Air fryer basket and then air fry for 7 minutes.
5. Dish out and serve warm.

Serving Suggestions: Serve with the warm vegetable salad.
Variation Tip: You can also make glaze with the maple syrup.
Per Serving: Calories: 342| Fat: 11g| Sat Fat: 2.9g| Carbohydrates: 34.7g|Fiber: 4.9g|Sugar: 12.1g|Protein: 27.9g

Crispy Cod

⏰ **Prep:** 10 minutes 🍲 **Cook:** 12 minutes 📚 **Serves:** 4

Ingredients:

¼ cup polenta
1 pound cod, about 1-inch thick, cut into 4 pieces
¼ cup all-purpose flour
1½ teaspoons garlic salt
½ teaspoon ground black pepper
Olive oil cooking spray
1½ teaspoons seafood seasoning
1 teaspoon onion powder
½ teaspoon paprika

Preparation:

1. Switch the temperature of the Air fryer to 195°C.
2. In a small bowl, merge the cod fillets with flour, polenta, seafood seasoning, onion powder, garlic salt, pepper, and paprika.
3. Spray the sides of cod with cooking spray. Layer the cod into the Air fryer basket and then air fry for 12 minutes, flipping once in between.
4. Dish out the cod and serve warm.

Serving Suggestions: Serve with sweet and sour coleslaw.
Variation Tip: You can use Old Bay seasoning.
Per Serving: Calories: 171 | Fat: 2g | Sat Fat: 0g | Carbohydrates: 15g | Fiber: 1g | Sugar: 1g | Protein: 23g

Crispy Tilapia Fillets

⏰ **Prep:** 5 minutes 🍲 **Cook:** 12 minutes 📚 **Serves:** 2

Ingredients:

¼ cup flour
1 tablespoon cornstarch
2 tilapia fillets
1 egg
¼ teaspoon salt and pepper
1 teaspoon paprika
3 tablespoons Old Bay seasoning
1 tablespoon water
Cooking spray

Preparation:

1. Switch the temperature of the Air fryer to 200°C.
2. In a small bowl, merge all the seasonings.
3. In a bowl, whisk eggs with water and in another bowl, spread flour.
4. Dip the tilapia in the egg mixture after dredging them in the flour mixture.
5. Coat with the seasonings mixture and layer the tilapia into the Air fryer basket.
6. Cook for 12 minutes, flipping once in between.
7. Dish out and serve warm.

Serving Suggestions: You can serve with tartar sauce or ketchup.
Variation Tip: You can also use butter instead of oil.
Per Serving: Calories: 149 | Fat: 5g | Sat Fat: 1g | Carbohydrates: 16g | Fiber: 1g | Sugar: 2.2g | Protein: 10g

Chapter 4 Fish and Seafood Recipes

Easy Air Fryer Salmon

⏱ **Prep: 5 minutes** 🍲 **Cook: 15 minutes** 🍽 **Serves: 4**

Ingredients:

1 teaspoon olive oil
1 lb. salmon fillet
1 teaspoon salt
Seasonings of choice
½ teaspoon pepper

Preparation:

1. Switch the temperature of the Air fryer to 180°C.
2. In a small bowl, merge the salmon fillets with olive oil, salt, and pepper.
3. Layer the salmon, skin side up into the Air fryer basket and then air fry for 15 minutes.
4. Dish out the salmon and serve warm.

Serving Suggestions: Serve topped with lemon wedges.
Variation Tip: You can also add celery instead of parsley.
Per Serving: Calories: 104 | Fat: 4.3g | Sat Fat: 0.2g | Carbohydrates: 0.2g | Fiber: 0g | Sugar: 0g | Protein: 16.4g

Garlicky Cod Loins

⏱ **Prep: 10 minutes** 🍲 **Cook: 10 minutes** 🍽 **Serves: 4**

Ingredients:

4 tablespoons butter, melted
4 cod loins
6 garlic cloves, minced
2 tablespoons fresh dill, chopped
2 tablespoons lemon juice
½ teaspoon salt

Preparation:

1. Switch the temperature of the Air fryer to 185°C.
2. In a small bowl, merge the cod fillets with butter, garlic, lemon juice, dill, and salt.
3. Layer the cod in the Air fryer basket and then air fry for 10 minutes.
4. Dish out the cod and serve warm.

Serving Suggestions: Serve with baked asparagus.
Variation Tip: You can also use more herbs.
Per Serving: Calories: 204 | Fat: 12.7g | Sat Fat: 7.5g | Carbohydrates: 2.5g | Fiber: 0.3g | Sugar: 0.2g | Protein: 20.8g

Crispy Anchovies with Lemon

⏰ **Prep:** 10 minutes   🍳 **Cook:** 6 minutes   🍽 **Serves:** 4

Ingredients:

1 cup all-purpose flour
1 pound blue anchovies
1 tablespoon kosher salt
1 lemon, cut into wedges
1 tablespoon peanut oil

Preparation:

1. Switch the temperature of the Air fryer to 175°C.
2. In a small bowl, merge the flour and salt.
3. Dredge the anchovies in the flour mixture.
4. Layer the anchovies into the Air fryer basket.
5. Cook for 6 minutes, flipping once in between.
6. Dish out and serve warm with lemon wedges.

Serving Suggestions: Serve with basil on top.
Variation Tip: Add red chili flakes to spice up the taste.
Per Serving: Calories: 493 | Fat: 24g | Sat Fat: 5g | Carbohydrates: 46g | Fiber: 6g | Sugar: 8g | Protein: 28g

Air Fryer Lemon Mackerel Fillets

⏰ **Prep:** 3 minutes   🍳 **Cook:** 10 minutes   🍽 **Serves:** 2

Ingredients:

⅓ teaspoons salt
2 mackerel fillets
Black pepper, to taste
1 pinch cumin
½ lemon
½ teaspoon garlic powder

Preparation:

1. Switch the temperature of the Air fryer to 200°C.
2. In a small bowl, dust the mackerel fillets with salt, pepper, cumin and garlic powder.
3. Layer the mackerel fillets over lemon slices into the Air fryer basket and then air fry for 10 minutes, flipping once in between.
4. Dish out and serve warm.

Serving Suggestions: Serve with pickled onions.
Variation Tip: You can use any fish of your choice.
Per Serving: Calories: 242 | Fat: 16g | Sat Fat: 4g | Carbohydrates: 3g | Fiber: 1g | Sugar: 1g | Protein: 21g

Air Fryer Kalamansi Tilapia

⏲ **Prep:** 5 minutes   🍲 **Cook:** 10 minutes   🍽 **Serves:** 2

Ingredients:

3 tablespoons kalamansi juice
1 tilapia, gutted and cleaned
Salt, to taste
Cooking oil spray
Seasoning powder, to taste

Preparation:

1. Switch the temperature of the Air fryer to 200°C.
2. Scrub the sides of tilapia with kalamansi juice and salt.
3. Shower the both sides of tilapia with cooking oil spray and dust with seasoning powder.
4. Layer the tilapia in Air fryer basket and then air fry for 10 minutes, flipping once in between.
5. Dish out the tilapia and serve warm.

Serving Suggestions: Serve garnished with chopped sage.
Variation Tip: You can use kalamansi instead of lemon.
Per Serving: Calories: 156 | Fat: 13g | Sat Fat: 2g | Carbohydrates: 2g | Fiber: 0.3g | Sugar: 0.8g | Protein: 19g

Baked Lemony Rainbow Trout

⏲ **Prep:** 5 minutes   🍲 **Cook:** 12 minutes   🍽 **Serves:** 4

Ingredients:

3 tablespoons olive oil
4 (4-oz) Rainbow trout fillets
2 teaspoons lemon juice
2 teaspoons fresh parsley
½ teaspoon paprika
¼ teaspoon black pepper
2 cloves garlic, minced
2 teaspoons fresh dill
¾ teaspoon sea salt
Thin lemon slices

Preparation:

1. Switch the temperature of the Air fryer to 200°C.
2. In a small bowl, merge the trout with olive oil, garlic, lemon juice, dill, parsley, and paprika.
3. Dust both sides of trout with sea salt and black pepper.
4. Layer the trout into the Air fryer basket and top with thin lemon slices.
5. Cook for 12 minutes and dish out to serve warm.

Serving Suggestions: Serve with balsamic onions.
Variation Tip: You can use any fresh herbs of your choice.
Per Serving: Calories: 271 | Fat: 21.4g | Sat Fat: 4.2g | Carbohydrates: 5.1g | Fiber: 0.3g | Sugar: 1.5g | Protein: 17.8g

Chapter 5 Chicken and Poultry Recipes

Chicken Wings with Blue Cheese Dressing

⏰ Prep: 10 minutes 🍲 Cook: 20 minutes 🍽 Serves: 4

Ingredients:

2 lbs. chicken wings
Nonstick cooking spray
Salt and black pepper, to taste
Blue Cheese Dressing (For Serving)
½ cup hot sauce
1 teaspoon Worcestershire sauce
4 tablespoons butter, melted
½ teaspoon garlic powder
¼ cup blue cheese, crumbled

Preparation:

1. Switch the temperature of the Air fryer to 195°C.
2. Dust the wings with salt and black pepper.
3. Grease the air fryer basket with cooking spray. Layer the wings in the Air fryer basket and then air fry for about 20 minutes, flipping once in between.
4. Meanwhile, in a large bowl, merge hot sauce, butter, Worcestershire sauce, blue cheese and garlic powder to make blue cheese dressing.
5. Add wings to the sauce and mix thoroughly.
6. Serve hot.

Serving Suggestions: You can serve it with tartar sauce.
Variation Tip: Add some red chili powder for extra spice.
Per Serving: Calories: 577 | Fat: 32.5g | Sat Fat: 12.7g | Carbohydrates: 1.6g | Fiber: 0.1g | Sugar: 0.9g | Protein: 66.3g

Spicy Chicken Wings

⏰ Prep: 5 minutes 🍲 Cook: 20 minutes 🍽 Serves: 4

Ingredients:

2 lbs. chicken wings
1 tablespoon olive oil
Seasoning
½ teaspoon black pepper
1 teaspoon paprika
½ teaspoon onion powder
¼ teaspoon baking powder
½ teaspoon garlic powder
Salt, to taste
Sauce
1 tablespoon butter
¾ cup hot sauce
1 teaspoon chili flakes
½ teaspoon garlic powder

Preparation:

1. Switch the temperature of the Air fryer to 195°C.
2. Dust the wings with oil and seasoning mix and marinate for 2 hours.
3. Layer the wings in the Air fryer basket and then air fry for about 20 minutes, flipping once in between.
4. Meanwhile, in a large bowl, merge all the sauce ingredients and cook for 10 minutes in a pan on low heat.
5. Add wings to the sauce and mix thoroughly.
6. Serve hot.

Serving Suggestions: Serve garnished with spring onions and coriander.
Variation Tip: You can add or omit spices according to your taste.
Per Serving: Calories: 467 | Fat: 19.9g | Sat Fat: 6.5g | Carbohydrates: 2.2g | Fiber: 1g | Sugar: 1g | Protein: 13g

Honey Mustard Glazed Chicken Wings

⏱ **Prep: 5 minutes** 🍲 **Cook: 20 minutes** 🍽 **Serves: 6**

Ingredients:

¼ cup Dijon mustard
12 chicken wings
3 tablespoons honey
½ teaspoon garlic powder
½ teaspoon kosher salt
2 tablespoons butter, unsalted
½ teaspoon cayenne pepper

Preparation:

1. Switch the temperature of the Air fryer to 200°C.
2. Layer the wings in the Air fryer basket and then air fry for about 20 minutes, flipping once in between.
3. Meanwhile, in a large bowl, merge Dijon mustard, honey, butter, cayenne pepper, garlic powder, and salt and cook for 10 minutes in a pan on low heat.
4. Add wings to the sauce and mix thoroughly.
5. Serve hot.

Serving Suggestions: Serve it with potato fries.
Variation Tip: You can also add some red chili flakes for more spiciness.
Per Serving: Calories: 624 | Fat: 40.3g | Sat Fat: 12.5g | Carbohydrates: 9.5g | Fiber: 0.4g | Sugar: 8.8g | Protein: 50.6g

Spicy Butterfly Chicken Drumsticks

⏱ **Prep: 5 minutes** 🍲 **Cook: 25 minutes** 🍽 **Serves: 3**

Ingredients:

1 tablespoon oil
6 chicken drumsticks
1 teaspoon paprika
1 teaspoon garlic powder
½ teaspoon salt
1 teaspoon Italian seasoning
½ teaspoon onion powder
¼ teaspoon cayenne pepper

Preparation:

1. Switch the temperature of the Air fryer to 200°C.
2. Cut the chicken drumsticks on one side to open like wings.
3. Dust the chicken with salt and seasoning, and brush olive oil over it.
4. Layer the chicken drumsticks in the Air fryer basket and then air fry for about 25 minutes, flipping once in between.
5. Dish out and serve warm.

Serving Suggestions: Serve topped with lemon wedges.
Variation Tip: You can also use butter instead of olive oil.
Per Serving: Calories: 289 | Fat: 19g | Sat Fat: 4g | Carbohydrates: 2g | Fiber: 1g | Sugar: 1g | Protein: 27g

Air Fryer Curry Chicken Drumsticks

⏰ **Prep: 35 minutes** 🍲 **Cook: 20 minutes** ◆ **Serves: 4**

Ingredients:

¾ teaspoon salt, divided
1 pound chicken drumsticks
2 tablespoons olive oil
½ teaspoon onion salt
Minced fresh cilantro, optional
2 teaspoons curry powder
½ teaspoon garlic powder

Preparation:

1. Switch the temperature of the Air fryer to 190°C.
2. Dissolve ½ teaspoon salt and some water to cover chicken legs.
3. Eliminate the legs from water and pat them dry.
4. In a bowl, merge the chicken legs with oil, onion salt, curry powder, garlic powder, and remaining ¼ teaspoon salt.
5. Layer the chicken legs in the Air fryer basket and then air fry for about 20 minutes, flipping once in between.
6. Dish out and serve garnished with cilantro.

Serving Suggestions: Serve with grilled potatoes and salad.
Variation Tip: You can add chili to increase spiciness.
Per Serving: Calories: 256 | Fat: 13.6g | Sat Fat: 2.7g | Carbohydrates: 0.9g | Fiber: 0.4g | Sugar: 0.1g | Protein: 31.4g

Spiced Chicken with Bird's Eye Chilies

⏰ **Prep: 40 minutes** 🍲 **Cook: 25 minutes** ◆ **Serves: 2**

Ingredients:

1 teaspoon ginger, grated
¾ lb. chicken thighs, chopped
1 teaspoon garlic, grated
¼ teaspoon white pepper
4 tablespoons cornstarch
2 stalks bird's eye chilies
¼ teaspoon salt
½ teaspoon sugar
2 stalks curry leaves
Oil spray
Seasoning Powder
½ teaspoon white pepper
½ teaspoon salt
¼ teaspoon five spice powder

Preparation:

1. Switch the temperature of the Air fryer to 180°C.
2. In a bowl, merge chicken thighs with ginger, garlic, salt, white pepper, and sugar. Marinate for 30 minutes.
3. Put curry leaves and bird's eye chilies in the Air fryer and then air fry for about 5 minutes.
4. Add cornstarch to the marinated chicken thighs until well-coated.
5. Layer the chicken in the Air fryer basket and then air fry for about 20 minutes, flipping once in between.
6. In a bowl, merge all the seasoning powder and add chicken and curry leaves.
7. Toss well and serve warm.

Serving Suggestions: Serve with potatoes and carrots.
Variation Tip: You can also make chicken breasts with this recipe.
Per Serving: Calories: 395 | Fat: 13g | Sat Fat: 3.6g | Carbohydrates: 16.3g | Fiber: 0.06g | Sugar: 0.1g | Protein: 49.5g

Simple Turkey Steaks

⏰ **Prep:** 5 minutes 🍳 **Cook:** 20 minutes 🍽 **Serves:** 4

Ingredients:

½ teaspoon salt
4 turkey breast steaks
½ teaspoon black
pepper
1 teaspoon olive oil
1 teaspoon Italian seasoning

Preparation:

1. Switch the temperature of the Air fryer to 200°C.
2. In a bowl, rub turkey steaks with salt, pepper and Italian seasoning, and brush olive oil over it.
3. Layer the turkey steaks in the Air fryer basket and then air fry for about 20 minutes, flipping once in between.
4. Dish out and serve warm.

Serving Suggestions: Serve with pickled vegetables.
Variation Tip: You can also use Old Bay seasoning.
Per Serving: Calories: 122 | Fat: 1g | Sat Fat: 1g | Carbohydrates: 1g | Fiber: 1g | Sugar: 1g | Protein: 28g

Crispy Turkey Escalope

⏰ **Prep:** 10 minutes 🍳 **Cook:** 25 minutes 🍽 **Serves:** 4

Ingredients:

2 turkey escalopes
3 tablespoons flour
2 eggs
¼ cup breadcrumbs

Preparation:

1. Switch the temperature of the Air fryer to 200°C.
2. In a small bowl, place breadcrumbs.
3. In another bowl, whisk eggs and in a third bowl, spread flour.
4. Dip the turkey in the egg mixture after dredging them in the flour mixture.
5. Coat with the breadcrumbs and layer the turkey into the Air fryer basket.
6. Cook for 25 minutes, flipping once in between.
7. Dish out and serve warm.

Serving Suggestions: Serve with spaghetti.
Variation Tip: You can also use chicken instead of turkey.
Per Serving: Calories: 137 | Fat: 3.7g | Sat Fat: 1.2g | Carbohydrates: 10g | Fiber: 0.7g | Sugar: 0.7g | Protein: 15.8g

Chapter 5 Chicken and Poultry Recipes

Crispy Parmesan Turkey Cutlets

Prep: 10 minutes **Cook: 25 minutes** **Serves: 2**

Ingredients:

1 large egg, beaten
½ cup panko bread crumbs
2 teaspoons lemon zest
½ teaspoon cayenne pepper
2 turkey breasts, boneless and skinless
¼ cup plain flour
¼ cup Parmesan, freshly grated
1 teaspoon dried oregano
Salt and black pepper, to taste

Preparation:

1. Switch the temperature of the Air fryer to 175°C.
2. In a small bowl, merge panko, Parmesan, lemon zest, oregano, cayenne, salt and pepper.
3. In another bowl, whisk eggs and in a third bowl, spread flour.
4. Dip the turkey in the egg mixture after dredging them in the flour mixture.
5. Coat with the breadcrumbs and layer the turkey into the Air fryer basket.
6. Cook for 25 minutes, flipping once in between.
7. Dish out and serve warm.

Serving Suggestions: Serve with crispy chips.
Variation Tip: You can also use almond flour instead of plain flour.
Per Serving: Calories: 294 | Fat: 8g | Sat Fat: 3.3g | Carbohydrates: 35g | Fiber: 2.4g | Sugar: 3.6g | Protein: 20.4g

Crispy Breaded Chicken Breasts

Prep: 10 minutes **Cook: 15 minutes** **Serves: 1**

Ingredients:

1 egg
1 large chicken breast
2 tablespoons flour
¼ teaspoon garlic powder
¼ teaspoon black pepper
1 cup breadcrumbs
½ teaspoon salt
1 teaspoon olive oil

Preparation:

1. Switch the temperature of the Air fryer to 180°C.
2. In a small bowl, merge flour with garlic powder, salt, and black pepper.
3. In another bowl, whisk eggs and in a third bowl, spread breadcrumbs.
4. Dip the chicken in the egg mixture after dredging them in the flour mixture.
5. Coat with the breadcrumbs and layer the chicken into the Air fryer basket.
6. Spray with oil and cook for 15 minutes, flipping once in between.
7. Dish out and serve warm.

Serving Suggestions: Serve with cream cheese.
Variation Tip: You can use either fine white breadcrumbs or panko breadcrumbs.
Per Serving: Calories: 585 | Fat: 12.9g | Sat Fat: 2.1g | Carbohydrates: 75.3g | Fiber: 2.3g | Sugar: 0.6g | Protein: 39.5g

Chapter 5 Chicken and Poultry Recipes

Cheese Turkey Meatballs

⏰ **Prep: 10 minutes** 🍲 **Cook: 12 minutes** 🍽 **Serves: 6**

Ingredients:

- 1 cup onion, finely chopped
- 1 large egg
- 1 lb. ground turkey
- 1 teaspoon garlic granules
- ½ cup panko breadcrumbs
- 1½ tablespoons mayonnaise, full-fat
- Salt and black pepper, to taste
- 1 tablespoon Italian seasoning
- ½ cup parmesan cheese, freshly grated
- Fresh parsley, to serve

Preparation:

1. Switch the temperature of the Air fryer to 175°C.
2. In a bowl, merge ground turkey with onions, egg, garlic granules, Italian seasoning, mayonnaise, breadcrumbs, parmesan cheese, salt, and black pepper.
3. Thoroughly mix and form balls with this mixture.
4. Layer the meatballs in the Air fryer basket and then air fry for about 12 minutes, flipping once in between.
5. Dish out and serve warm.

Serving Suggestions: Serve with zucchini noodles
Variation Tip: You can use pork rinds instead of breadcrumbs.
Per Serving: Calories: 243 | Fat: 13.3g | Sat Fat: 3.3g | Carbohydrates: 8.6g | Fiber: 1.2g | Sugar: 1.5g | Protein: 25.7g

Air Fryer Chicken Meatballs

⏰ **Prep: 10 minutes** 🍲 **Cook: 10 minutes** 🍽 **Serves: 6**

Ingredients:

- 1 egg
- 1 lb. ground chicken
- ½ cup breadcrumbs panko
- 1 tablespoon olive oil
- 1 teaspoon onion powder
- ½ teaspoon salt
- 1 tablespoon dried parsley
- 3 tablespoons parmesan cheese, grated
- 1 teaspoon garlic powder
- 1 teaspoon paprika
- ½ teaspoon black pepper

Preparation:

1. Switch the temperature of the Air fryer to 200°C.
2. In a bowl, merge ground chicken, egg, bread crumbs, parmesan cheese, garlic powder, paprika, onion powder, olive oil, parsley, salt, and black pepper.
3. Thoroughly mix and form balls with this mixture.
4. Layer the meatballs in the Air fryer basket and then air fry for about 10 minutes, flipping once in between.
5. Dish out and serve warm.

Serving Suggestions: Serve with orange wedges and pomegranate arils.
Variation Tip: You can also make chicken breast with this recipe.
Per Serving: Calories: 207 | Fat: 9.2g | Sat Fat: 2.3g | Carbohydrates: 6.1g | Fiber: 0.9g | Sugar: 0.5g | Protein: 24.2g

Garlicky Turkey Breast with Herbs

⏱ **Prep: 5 minutes**   🍲 **Cook: 50 minutes**   ≋ **Serves: 4**

Ingredients:

- 3 tablespoons olive oil
- 1 (4 lbs.) turkey breast
- 2 tablespoons garlic, minced
- 1 teaspoon thyme
- 1 teaspoon kosher salt
- 1 teaspoon rosemary
- 1 teaspoon basil

Preparation:

1. Switch the temperature of the Air fryer to 160°C.
2. In a bowl, merge the turkey breast with oil, herbs and garlic.
3. Layer the turkey breast in the Air fryer basket and then air fry for about
4. 50 minutes, flipping once in between.
5. Dish out and serve warm.

Serving Suggestions: Serve with roasted garlic and onions.
Variation Tip: You can use also use garlic powder instead of garlic.
Per Serving: Calories: 570 | Fat: 18.1g | Sat Fat: 3g | Carbohydrates: 20.9g | Fiber: 2.6g | Sugar: 16g | Protein: 77.7g

Paprika Chicken Thighs

⏱ **Prep: 10 minutes**   🍲 **Cook: 20 minutes**   ≋ **Serves: 6**

Ingredients:

- 1 tablespoon paprika
- 2 lbs. chicken thighs
- ⅛ teaspoon oregano
- ½ teaspoon brown sugar
- ¼ teaspoon garlic granules
- Salt, to taste
- ½ teaspoon parsley
- ½ teaspoon cayenne
- ¼ teaspoon onion powder
- 1 tablespoon sunflower oil

Preparation:

1. Switch the temperature of the Air fryer to 180°C.
2. In a bowl, merge the chicken pieces with all the remaining ingredients and marinate for an hour.
3. Layer the chicken thighs in the Air fryer basket and then air fry for about 20 minutes, flipping once in between.
4. Dish out and serve warm.

Serving Suggestions: Serve with stir fried veggies.
Variation Tip: You can make this recipe with turkey thighs too.
Per Serving: Calories: 192 | Fat: 15g | Sat Fat: 4g | Carbohydrates: 1g | Fiber: 1g | Sugar: 1g | Protein: 12g

Easy Air Fryer Chicken Breasts

⏰ **Prep: 5 minutes** 🍲 **Cook: 20 minutes** 🍽 **Serves: 2**

Ingredients:

1 teaspoon paprika	pepper
2 chicken breasts	Salt, to taste
½ teaspoon parsley	¼ teaspoon garlic powder
¼ teaspoon black	½ tablespoon vegetable oil

Preparation:

1. Switch the temperature of the Air fryer to 200°C.
2. In a bowl, merge the chicken pieces with paprika, parsley, garlic powder, salt, black pepper, and vegetable oil and marinate for an hour.
3. Layer the marinated chicken breasts in the Air fryer basket and then air fry for about 20 minutes, flipping once in between.
4. Dish out and serve warm.

Serving Suggestions: Serve with white rice.
Variation Tip: You can also use bell peppers of your choice.
Per Serving: Calories: 290 | Fat: 9g | Sat Fat: 2g | Carbohydrates: 1g | Fiber: 1g | Sugar: 1g | Protein: 48g

Air Fryer Spiced Chicken with Vegetables

⏰ **Prep: 10 minutes** 🍲 **Cook: 15 minutes** 🍽 **Serves: 4**

Ingredients:

1 small head broccoli, chopped	1 small yellow bell pepper, chopped
1 lb. chicken thighs, boneless, chopped	1 tablespoon paprika
1 small red bell pepper, chopped	1 teaspoon black pepper
1 small red onion	1 tablespoon olive oil
1 tablespoon parsley	
Salt, to taste	
½ teaspoon garlic granules	

Preparation:

1. Switch the temperature of the Air fryer to 175°C.
2. Dust the chicken with half the pepper, salt, olive oil, paprika, parsley, and garlic. Mix well.
3. Merge the vegetables with remaining black pepper, parsley, paprika, garlic, salt, and olive oil and thoroughly mix.
4. Layer the chicken and vegetables in the Air fryer basket and then air fry for about 15 minutes.
5. Dish out and serve warm.

Serving Suggestions: Serve over rice.
Variation Tip: You can use vegetables of your choice.
Per Serving: Calories: 349 | Fat: 20g | Sat Fat: 6g | Carbohydrates: 16g | Fiber: 5g | Sugar: 5g | Protein: 28g

Spiced Whole Duck

⏱ **Prep: 15 minutes**　🍳 **Cook: 1 hour 40 minutes**　🍽 **Serves: 4**

Ingredients:

1½ teaspoons kosher salt
1 (4 pounds) whole duck
1 tablespoon dried parsley
2 teaspoons onion powder
3 teaspoons Cajun seasoning
2 teaspoons ginger powder
4 teaspoons dried basil
3 teaspoons paprika
3 teaspoons garlic powder
1 tablespoon olive oil

Preparation:

1. Switch the temperature of the Air fryer to 160°C.
2. In a bowl, merge all the seasonings and apply to the duck inside out.
3. Position the duck on the Air fryer basket.
4. Cook for about 1 hour 40 minutes, flipping once in between.
5. Dish out and serve warm.

Serving Suggestions: Serve with coleslaw.
Variation Tip: You can also use any other variety of apples.
Per Serving: Calories: 437 | Fat: 36g | Sat Fat: 12g | Carbohydrates: 5g | Fiber: 2g | Sugar: 1.1g | Protein: 23g

Chicken and Veggie Skewers

⏱ **Prep: 10 minutes**　🍳 **Cook: 10 minutes**　🍽 **Serves: 6**

Ingredients:

⅓ cup sweet chili sauce
1 lb. boneless skinless chicken breast, cut into bite sizes pieces
½ tablespoon Herbs de Provence
½ teaspoon red pepper flakes
1 teaspoon garlic granules
3 bell peppers, chopped
1 large onion, chopped
1 teaspoon smoked paprika
2 tablespoons vegetable oil
Salt and black pepper, to taste
1 zucchini, chopped

Preparation:

1. Switch the temperature of the Air fryer to 200°C.
2. Merge the chicken pieces with salt, black pepper, red pepper flakes.
3. Add zucchini, bell peppers, onions, smoked paprika, herbs de Provence, sweet chili sauce, and vegetable oil, and thoroughly mix.
4. Marinate well for about half an hour, then thread chicken and vegetables on the skewers.
5. Layer the chicken skewers in the Air fryer basket and then air fry for about 10 minutes, flipping once in between.
6. Dish out and serve warm.

Serving Suggestions: You can serve with carrots and peas.
Variation Tip: You can use herbs of your choice.
Per Serving: Calories: 191 | Fat: 7g | Sat Fat: 4g | Carbohydrates: 14g | Fiber: 2g | Sugar: 1.5g | Protein: 18g

Chicken-Avocado Patties

⏲ **Prep: 5 minutes** 🍲 **Cook: 20 minutes** 🍽 **Serves: 4**

Ingredients:

1 large egg
1 lb. ground lean chicken
½ tablespoon Cajun seasoning
2 tablespoons fresh parsley, chopped
Salt and pepper, to taste
½ tablespoon onion powder
⅓ cup avocado pulp
1 tablespoon Worcestershire sauce

Preparation:

1. Switch the temperature of the Air fryer to 180°C.
2. In a bowl, merge the ground chicken with Cajun seasoning, avocado, Worcestershire sauce, egg, onion powder, parsley, salt and pepper.
3. Thoroughly mix and form into patties.
4. Layer the burger patties in the Air fryer basket and then air fry for about 20 minutes, flipping once in between.
5. Dish out and serve warm.

Serving Suggestions: Serve with salad or inside buns.
Variation Tip: You can also add spices of your choice.
Per Serving: Calories: 200 | Fat: 9.6g | Sat Fat: 2.9g | Carbohydrates: 2.7g | Fiber: 0.9g | Sugar: 1.2g | Protein: 25g

Cumin Boneless Chicken Thighs

⏲ **Prep: 5 minutes** 🍲 **Cook: 18 minutes** 🍽 **Serves: 4**

Ingredients:
1 tablespoon smoked paprika
6 chicken thighs, boneless and skinless
½ teaspoon red pepper flakes
½ teaspoon sage
1 teaspoon dried parsley
2 tablespoons olive oil
1 tablespoon Worcestershire sauce
Salt and pepper, to taste
1 teaspoon garlic powder
1 teaspoon onion powder
¼ teaspoon cumin

Preparation:
1. Switch the temperature of the Air fryer to 195°C.
2. In a bowl, merge the chicken pieces with smoked paprika, onion powder, garlic powder, sage, red pepper flakes, parsley, cumin, salt, and black pepper.
3. Add in the olive oil and Worcestershire sauce, and marinate for about an hour.
4. Layer the chicken thighs in the Air fryer basket and then air fry for about 18 minutes, flipping once in between.
5. Dish out and serve warm.

Serving Suggestions: Serve with mashed potatoes or mushy peas.
Variation Tip: You can substitute olive oil with any flavorless oil.
Per Serving: Calories: 278 | Fat: 14g | Sat Fat: 3g | Carbohydrates: 3g | Fiber: 1g | Sugar: 1g | Protein: 33g

Chapter 6 Beef, Pork and Lamb Recipes

Easy Beef Burgers

⏰ **Prep: 2 minutes** 🍲 **Cook: 15 minutes** 📚 **Serves: 4**

Ingredients:

4 beef burger patties

Preparation:

1. Switch the temperature of the Air fryer to 200°C.
2. Layer the burger patties in the Air fryer basket and then air fry for about 15 minutes, flipping once in between.
3. Dish out and serve warm.

Serving Suggestions: Serve topped with cheese and inside the buns.
Variation Tip: You can add more spices if desired.
Per Serving: Calories: 197 | Fat: 12g | Sat Fat: 5g | Carbohydrates: 0g | Fiber: 0 g | Sugar: 0g | Protein: 21g

Herbed Steak Bites

⏰ **Prep: 5 minutes** 🍲 **Cook: 12 minutes** 📚 **Serves: 4**

Ingredients:

2 tablespoons olive oil
2 lbs. steak, cut into small pieces
1 teaspoon garlic powder
Salt and cracked pepper, to taste
½ teaspoon Herbs de Provence

Preparation:

1. Switch the temperature of the Air fryer to 200°C.
2. Dust the steak bites with herb de Provence, garlic powder, salt, black pepper, olive oil and thoroughly mix.
3. Layer the steak bites in the Air fryer basket and then air fry for about 12 minutes, flipping once in between.
4. Dish out and serve tossed with garlic butter.

Serving Suggestions: Serve with pickled onions.
Variation Tip: You can replace herb de Provence with any other herbs of choice.
Per Serving: Calories: 536 | Fat: 39g | Sat Fat: 15g | Carbohydrates: 1g | Fiber: 1g | Sugar: 1g | Protein: 46g

Air Fryer Steaks with Sweet Potatoes & Mushrooms

⏰ **Prep: 10 minutes** 🍲 **Cook: 35 minutes** 🍽 **Serves: 6**

Ingredients:

¼ cup crème Fraîche
1 lb. sweet potatoes, peeled, cut into wedges
1 tablespoon milk
2 teaspoons fresh tarragon, chopped
1 small green shallot, finely chopped
4 large flat mushrooms
1 tablespoon horseradish sauce
2 (225g) porterhouse steaks
¼ cup garlic butter, chopped
1 tablespoon olive oil

Preparation:

1. Switch the temperature of the Air fryer to 180°C.
2. In a bowl, merge crème Fraîche with milk, shallot, horseradish sauce, and garlic butter.
3. Position the sweet potatoes in the Air fryer basket and then air fry for about 20 minutes, flipping once in between.
4. Dish out and keep aside.
5. Layer the steaks in the Air fryer basket and then air fry for about 10 minutes, flipping once in between.
6. Dish out and keep aside with sweet potatoes.
7. Layer the mushrooms in the Air fryer basket and sprinkle with butter, oil, and tarragon.
8. Cook for about 5 minutes, flipping once in between.
9. Dish out with steak, sweet potatoes and mushrooms and serve drizzled with crème fraîche mixture.

Serving Suggestions: Serve with watercress.
Variation Tip: You can also use red potatoes instead of sweet potatoes.
Per Serving: Calories: 312 | Fat: 16.3g | Sat Fat: 6.6g | Carbohydrates: 17.9g | Fiber: 2.7g | Sugar: 5.3g | Protein: 22.8g

Easy Air Fryer Porterhouse Steaks

⏰ **Prep: 2 minutes** 🍲 **Cook: 10 minutes** 🍽 **Serves: 2**

Ingredients:

2 (225g) porterhouse steaks
1 teaspoon olive oil
Salt and black pepper, to taste

Preparation:

1. Switch the temperature of the Air fryer to 160°C.
2. In a bowl, rub the steaks with olive oil, salt and black pepper.
3. Layer the steaks in the Air fryer basket and then air fry for about 10 minutes, flipping once in between.
4. Dish out in a platter and serve warm.

Serving Suggestions: Serve with roasted garlic and chili.
Variation Tip: You can use coconut aminos instead of soy sauce.
Per Serving: Calories: 477 | Fat: 24g | Sat Fat: 9.2g | Carbohydrates: 0g | Fiber: 0g | Sugar: 0g | Protein: 61.2g

Chapter 6 Beef, Pork and Lamb Recipes

Pork Belly with Golden Syrup Sauce

⏱ **Prep: 15 minutes** 🍳 **Cook: 20 minutes** 🍽 **Serves: 8**

Ingredients:

- 1 tablespoon brown sugar
- 2 lbs. pork belly, boneless
- 3 teaspoons smoked paprika
- 1 teaspoon onion powder
- 1 teaspoon olive oil
- 2 teaspoons plain flour
- ½ teaspoon garlic powder

Golden Syrup Sauce
- 2 tablespoons golden syrup
- ¼ cup butter
- 2 tablespoons barbecue sauce
- 2 teaspoons Sriracha
- 1 tablespoon bourbon

Preparation:

1. Switch the temperature of the Air fryer to 200°C.
2. In a bowl, merge sugar, paprika, flour, oil, onion, and garlic powder.
3. Layer the pork belly in the Air fryer basket and then air fry for about 20 minutes, flipping once in between.
4. Meanwhile, merge butter, golden syrup, barbecue sauce, bourbon, and Sriracha to make the golden syrup sauce.
5. Transfer the sauce into a pan and simmer for about 7 minutes.
6. Dish out the pork belly bites and serve drizzled with golden syrup sauce.

Serving Suggestions: Serve with pickled vegetables.
Variation Tip: You can use garlic instead of garlic powder.
Per Serving: Calories: 611 | Fat: 36.5g | Sat Fat: 16.8g | Carbohydrates: 8g | Fiber: 0.4g | Sugar: 3.7g | Protein: 52.7g

Tasty Rib-Eye Steak

⏱ **Prep: 15 minutes** 🍳 **Cook: 10 minutes** 🍽 **Serves: 2**

Ingredients:

- 1 teaspoon paprika
- 2 ribeye steak
- ½ teaspoon oregano
- Salt, to taste
- ½ teaspoon black pepper

Preparation:

1. Switch the temperature of the Air fryer to 200°C.
2. In a bowl, merge steaks with paprika, oregano, salt, and black pepper. Mix well.
3. Layer the steaks in the Air fryer basket and then air fry for about 10 minutes, flipping once in between.
4. Dish out in a platter and serve warm.

Serving Suggestions: Serve with garlic herb butter.
Variation Tip: You can use any cut of steak, sirloin, or tri-tip.
Per Serving: Calories: 581 | Fat: 43g | Sat Fat: 21g | Carbohydrates: 2g | Fiber: 1g | Sugar: 1g | Protein: 46g

Chapter 6 Beef, Pork and Lamb Recipes

Sweet & Sour Flank Steak

⏲ **Prep: 5 minutes** 🍳 **Cook: 10 minutes** 🍽 **Serves: 4**

Ingredients:

1½ lbs. Flank Steak
¼ cup balsamic dressing
1 teaspoon ground garlic
½ teaspoon red pepper flakes
¼ cup soy sauce, low sodium
¼ cup brown sugar
2 tablespoons Worcestershire sauce
Salt and pepper, to taste

Preparation:

1. Switch the temperature of the Air fryer to 200°C.
2. In a bowl, merge steaks with all other ingredients. Mix well.
3. Layer the steaks in the Air fryer basket and then air fry for about 10 minutes, flipping once in between.
4. Dish out in a platter and serve warm.

Serving Suggestions: Serve with roasted asparagus.
Variation Tip: You can also serve with your favorite sauce.
Per Serving: Calories: 409 | Fat: 16.8g | Sat Fat: 5.9g | Carbohydrates: 12.6g | Fiber: 0.2g | Sugar: 10.6g | Protein: 48.4g

Homemade Beef Jerky

⏲ **Prep: 5 minutes** 🍳 **Cook: 20 minutes** 🍽 **Serves: 4**

Ingredients:

1 lb. beef sirloin steak, thinly sliced into strips
Marinade
½ cup Worcestershire sauce
1 tablespoon honey
½ teaspoon chili flakes
½ cup soy sauce
1 teaspoon onion powder

Preparation:

1. Switch the temperature of the Air fryer to 180°C.
2. In a bowl, merge the beef slices with all the marinade ingredients. Mix well.
3. Layer the beef strips in the Air fryer basket and then air fry for about 20 minutes, flipping once in between.
4. Dish out in a platter and serve warm.

Serving Suggestions: Serve with roasted veggies.
Variation Tip: You can also use maple syrup instead of honey.
Per Serving: Calories: 276 | Fat: 7.1g | Sat Fat: 2.7g | Carbohydrates: 13.3g | Fiber: 0.3g | Sugar: 11.1g | Protein: 36.5g

Mustard Pork Chops with Potatoes

⏰ **Prep: 15 minutes**   🍲 **Cook: 25 minutes**   🍽 **Serves: 4**

Ingredients:

- 1½ teaspoons olive oil
- 12 baby potatoes, halved
- 2 teaspoons honey
- ½ teaspoon ground paprika
- 2 teaspoons fresh thyme leaves
- 1 teaspoon Dijon mustard
- 4 pork cutlets

Preparation:

1. Switch the temperature of the Air fryer to 185°C.
2. In a bowl, merge pork chops with oil, honey, mustard and paprika. Mix well.
3. Layer the potatoes in the Air fryer basket and then air fry for about 10 minutes, flipping once in between.
4. Now, add pork chops to the Air fryer and cook for 12 minutes, tossing once in between.
5. Dish out and serve sprinkled with thyme.

Serving Suggestions: Serve with potatoes and steamed broccolini.
Variation Tip: You can also use your favorite rolls for serving.
Per Serving: Calories: 331 | Fat: 7.1g | Sat Fat: 1.3g | Carbohydrates: 56.2g | Fiber: 4.1g | Sugar: 3.4g | Protein: 9.4g

Herb Roast Beef

⏰ **Prep: 5 minutes**   🍲 **Cook: 30 minutes**   🍽 **Serves: 4**

Ingredients:

- 1 teaspoon black pepper
- 2 teaspoons coarse salt
- **For the Roast Beef**
- 3 tablespoons olive oil
- ½ teaspoon dried thyme
- ½ teaspoon dried rosemary
- ½ teaspoon garlic granules
- ½ teaspoon brown sugar
- 2½ oz. roasting beef joint

Preparation:

1. Switch the temperature of the Air fryer to 200°C.
2. In a bowl, merge the beef with all the seasoning ingredients.
3. Layer the beef in the Air fryer basket and then air fry for about 15 minutes, flipping once in between.
4. Switch the temperature of the Air fryer to 175°C.
5. Cook for about 15 minutes and dish out to serve.

Serving Suggestions: Serve with steamed broccoli.
Variation Tip: You can also use mustard powder instead of brown sugar.
Per Serving: Calories: 125 | Fat: 11g | Sat Fat: 2g | Carbohydrates: 2g | Fiber: 1g | Sugar: 1g | Protein: 4g

Chapter 6 Beef, Pork and Lamb Recipes

Air Fryer Mustard Pork Tenderloin

⏱ **Prep: 30 minutes**   🍳 **Cook: 30 minutes**   🍽 **Serves: 3**

Ingredients:

1 pork tenderloin
For the Glaze
1 tablespoon Dijon Mustard
2 tablespoons brown sugar
1 teaspoon paprika
1 teaspoon onion powder
¼ teaspoon black pepper
¼ teaspoon salt
½ teaspoon garlic powder
1 teaspoon Frank's Red Hot sauce

Preparation:

1. Switch the temperature of the Air fryer to 195°C.
2. In a bowl, merge the pork tenderloin with all the remaining ingredients. Marinate well.
3. Layer the pork chops in the Air fryer basket and then air fry for about 30 minutes, flipping once in between.
4. Dish out in a platter and serve warm.

Serving Suggestions: Serve with red radishes.
Variation Tip: You can also use red chili flakes for added spiciness.
Per Serving: Calories: 175 | Fat: 4.1g | Sat Fat: 1.4g | Carbohydrates: 3.8g | Fiber: 0.3g | Sugar: 3.2g | Protein: 29.3g

Simple Pork Steaks

⏱ **Prep: 5 minutes**   🍳 **Cook: 10 minutes**   🍽 **Serves: 4**

Ingredients:

1 tablespoon vegetable oil
4 pork steaks, about 1 inch thick
1½ tablespoons pork seasoning
Salt and black pepper, to taste

Preparation:

1. Switch the temperature of the Air fryer to 200°C.
2. In a bowl, dust both sides of the pork steaks with pork rub, salt and black pepper, and scrub with oil.
3. Layer the pork steaks in the Air fryer basket and then air fry for about 10 minutes, flipping once in between.
4. Dish out in a platter and serve warm.

Serving Suggestions: Serve over cooked rice.
Variation Tip: You can substitute vegetable oil with any other flavorless cooking oil.
Per Serving: Calories: 200 | Fat: 11.4g | Sat Fat: 3.7g | Carbohydrates: 0g | Fiber: 0g | Sugar: 0g | Protein: 22g

Easy Air Fryer Lamb Steaks

⏱ **Prep: 5 minutes** 🍲 **Cook: 12 minutes** 📚 **Serves: 2**

Ingredients:

2 lamb steaks, 1-inch thick
1 teaspoon salt and black pepper
½ tablespoon light olive oil

Preparation:

1. Switch the temperature of the Air fryer to 200°C.
2. In a bowl, dust the lamb steaks with salt and black pepper, and scrub with oil.
3. Layer the lamb steaks in the Air fryer basket and then air fry for about 12 minutes, flipping once in between.
4. Dish out in a platter and serve warm.

Serving Suggestions: Serve with piccalilli or your favorite pickle.
Variation Tip: You can use any seasoning of your choice.
Per Serving: Calories: 469 | Fat: 31g | Sat Fat: 11g | Carbohydrates: 0g | Fiber: 0g | Sugar: 0g | Protein: 43g

Delicious Marinated Pork Chops

⏱ **Prep: 10 minutes** 🍲 **Cook: 12 minutes** 📚 **Serves: 4**

Ingredients:

4 (8-oz) Pork chops, boneless
Marinade:
¼ cup coconut aminos
⅓ cup olive oil
1 tablespoon lemon juice
4 cloves garlic, pressed
¾ teaspoon sea salt
1 tablespoon Dijon mustard
½ teaspoon black pepper

Preparation:

1. Switch the temperature of the Air fryer to 200°C.
2. In a bowl, merge the pork chops with all the marinade ingredients. Marinate well.
3. Layer the pork chops in the Air fryer basket and then air fry for about 12 minutes, flipping once in between.
4. Dish out in a platter and serve warm.

Serving Suggestions: Serve with roasted broccoli.
Variation Tip: You can also use almond flour.
Per Serving: Calories: 893 | Fat: 73.4g | Sat Fat: 23.6g | Carbohydrates: 4.5g | Fiber: 0.3g | Sugar: 0.1g | Protein: 58.4g

Herbed Lamb Ribs

⏰ **Prep: 10 minutes** 🍲 **Cook: 10 minutes** 🍽 **Serves: 8**

Ingredients:

8 lamb ribs
For Seasoning:
¼ cup olive oil
1 teaspoon thyme
2 garlic cloves, minced
1 teaspoon rosemary
1 teaspoon oregano
Salt and black pepper, to taste

Preparation:

1. Switch the temperature of the Air fryer to 150°C.
2. In a bowl, merge all the seasoning ingredients and coat over lamb ribs.
3. Layer the lamb ribs in the Air fryer basket and then air fry for about 10 minutes, flipping once in between.
4. Dish out in a platter and serve warm.

Serving Suggestions: Serve with vegetable sauté or salads.
Variation Tip: You can also use seasoning of your choice.
Per Serving: Calories: 425 | Fat: 27.5g | Sat Fat: 8.5g | Carbohydrates: 0.6g | Fiber: 0.2g | Sugar: 0g | Protein: 41.7g

Macadamia Crusted Rack of Lamb

⏰ **Prep: 20 minutes** 🍲 **Cook: 30 minutes** 🍽 **Serves: 8**

Ingredients:

1 garlic clove
2 lbs. rack of lamb
Salt and black pepper, to taste
1 tablespoon fresh rosemary, chopped
1 tablespoon olive oil
½ cup macadamia nuts, unsalted
1 tablespoon breadcrumbs
1 egg

Preparation:

1. Switch the temperature of the Air fryer to 180°C.
2. Merge olive oil and garlic and rub rack of lamb with this garlic oil, further seasoning it with salt and black pepper.
3. In a bowl, merge all the nuts, breadcrumbs, and rosemary.
4. In another bowl, whisk egg and dip the lamb rack in it.
5. Coat the macadamia crust over rack of lamb.
6. Layer the rack of lamb in the Air fryer basket and then air fry for about 30 minutes, flipping once in between.
7. Dish out in a platter and serve warm.

Serving Suggestions: Serve with Brussels sprouts.
Variation Tip: You can replace the macadamia nuts with hazelnuts, cashews, and pistachios.
Per Serving: Calories: 279 | Fat: 18.8g | Sat Fat: 5g | Carbohydrates: 2.2g | Fiber: 0.9g | Sugar: 0.5g | Protein: 24.6g

Herbed Lamb Chops with Garlic Sauce

⏲ **Prep: 15 minutes** 🍱 **Cook: 22 minutes** 🍽 **Serves: 4**

Ingredients:

- 3 tablespoons olive oil
- 1 garlic bulb
- 1 tablespoon fresh oregano, finely chopped
- 8 lamb chops
- Sea salt and black pepper, to taste

Preparation:

1. Switch the temperature of the Air fryer to 200°C.
2. Position the garlic bulb in the Air fryer basket and coat with olive oil.
3. Cook for about 12 minutes and keep aside.
4. In a bowl, merge herbs, sea salt, pepper and olive oil.
5. Coat half of the herb oil mixture over the lamb chops.
6. Mix the remaining herb oil mixture with garlic.
7. Layer the lamb chops in the Air fryer basket and then air fry for about 10 minutes, flipping once in between.
8. Dish out in a platter and serve with garlic sauce.

Serving Suggestions: Serve with couscous and braised zucchini.
Variation Tip: You can use pork chops instead of lamb chops.
Per Serving: Calories: 706 | Fat: 34.6g | Sat Fat: 10.1g | Carbohydrates: 1.5g | Fiber: 0.5g | Sugar: 0.1g | Protein: 91.9g

Rack of lamb with Mint Pesto

⏲ **Prep: 15 minutes** 🍱 **Cook: 15 minutes** 🍽 **Serves: 4**

Ingredients:

- 1 bunch fresh mint
- 2 racks of lamb
- 2 garlic cloves
- 1 tablespoon honey
- ¼ cup olive oil, extra virgin
- Salt and black pepper, to taste

Preparation:

1. Switch the temperature of the Air fryer to 200°C.
2. In a blender, blitz mint, garlic, oil, and honey, salt and black pepper to form mint pesto.
3. Merge the rack of lamb with mint pesto. Marinate well.
4. Layer the rack of lamb in the Air fryer basket and then air fry for about 15 minutes, flipping once in between.
5. Dish out in a platter and serve warm.

Serving Suggestions: Serve with mashed potatoes and fresh vegetables.
Variation Tip: You can also use maple syrup instead of honey.
Per Serving: Calories: 440 | Fat: 24.8g | Sat Fat: 6.1g | Carbohydrates: 6.8g | Fiber: 1.6g | Sugar: 4.3g | Protein: 46.8g

Chapter 6 Beef, Pork and Lamb Recipes

Chapter 7 Dessert Recipes

Pear, Blackberry and Pistachio Crumble

⏱ Prep: 10 minutes 🍲 Cook: 35 minutes 🍽 Servies: 4

Ingredients:

4 large ripe pears, peeled and cubed
1 cup blackberry
1 cup golden granulated sugar
1 cup unsalted butter, cold, cut into small pieces
1 cup shelled pistachio, roughly chopped
1 cup plain flour
½ cup demerara sugar
ice cream, to serve (optional)
Salt, to taste

Preparation:

1. Switch the air-fryer to 175°C and preheat for 10 minutes.
2. In a saucepan, cook sugar and pears until soft. Add blackberries and wait until the mixture boils.
3. Divide the fruit mixture into the ramekins and set aside.
4. Mix butter, flour, and salt in a bowl until the mixture is crumbly. Add sugar and pistachios and mix well.
5. Sprinkle the crumble mixture over the filled ramekins. Freeze it for one hour and then cook it in the air fryer for about 35 minutes or until it turns golden brown.
6. Serve warm, and enjoy.

Serving Suggestions: serve with vanilla ice cream
Variation Tip: You can also use hazelnuts instead of pistachios.
Per Serving: Calories: 768 | Fat: 33g | Sat Fat: 15g | Carbohydrates: 115g | Fiber: 0g | Sugar: 76g | Protein: 10g

Raspberry Cupcakes

⏱ Prep: 30 minutes 🍲 Cook: 20 minutes 🍽 Servies: 12

Ingredients:

⅓ cup butter, softened
1½ cups plain flour
1 teaspoon vanilla extract
5 eggs, 4 separated
1½ cups golden or white caster sugar
1 teaspoon baking powder
5 fl oz. milk
12 teaspoons raspberry jam
¼ cup raspberries

Preparation:

1. Switch the air fryer to 150°C and preheat for 10 minutes.
2. Line a 6-hole cupcake pan with the cupcake liners and set aside.
3. Beat sugar and butter until fluffy. Add vanilla extract, an egg, and four egg yolks and beat well to combine.
4. Add flour, baking powder, and milk to the egg mixture.
5. Fill cupcake liners with cake mixture until it is half filled. Add 1 teaspoon of jam to each cupcake mixture. Fill the cupcake batter until it is filled ⅔rd. Smooth out the top.
6. Bake in the air fryer for 20 minutes.
7. Meanwhile, prepare meringue by beating egg whites with 1 cup of granulated sugar until stiff peaks form.
8. Pipe meringue on the cupcakes and color them with the blow torch. Garnish with raspberry and serve.

Serving Suggestions: Serve with tea
Variation Tip: If you don't have a blow torch, you can air fry the meringue for 10 minutes until it is firm.
Per Serving: Calories: 374 | Fat: 20g | Sat Fat: 12g | Carbohydrates: 47g | Fiber: 1g | Sugar: 36g | Protein: 6g

Maple Pears with Roasted Pecan Nuts

⏱ **Prep:** 5 minutes 🍳 **Cook:** 25 minutes ❖ **Servies:** 4

Ingredients:

4 ripe pears
2 tablespoons maple syrup, plus extra to serve
2oz pecan nuts, broken roughly

Preparation:

1. Switch the air fryer to 40°C and preheat for 5 minutes.
2. Core pears and cut them in half. Place them into a dish along with maple syrup. Cover with foil and bake in the air fryer for 20 minutes.
3. Pears should be soft by then. Once cooked, set it aside.
4. Roast pecans in the air fryer for 4 minutes. Remove and coarsely chop them.
5. Sprinkle on pears and serve.

Serving Suggestions: serve with Greek yoghurt
Variation Tip: You can use hazelnuts as well. Sprinkle cinnamon on the pears for variation in taste.
Per Serving: Calories: 209 | Fat: 9g | Sat Fat: 1g | Carbohydrates: 32g | Fiber: 4g | Sugar: 9g | Protein: 2g

Banana Bread with Vanilla Ricotta & Raspberries Compote

⏱ **Prep:** 30 minutes 🍳 **Cook:** 30 minutes ❖ **Servies:** 8

Ingredients:

For the Banana Bread
2-3 very ripe bananas (mashed)
⅔ cup butter, softened
⅔ cup light muscovado sugar
2 large eggs
¼ teaspoon lemon zest
1 teaspoon vanilla extract
¾ cup buttermilk
2½ cups self-raising flour
1 teaspoon ground cinnamon
½ teaspoon bicarbonate of soda

For the Vanilla Ricotta
9 oz. tub of ricotta
3 teaspoons vanilla bean paste
juice of 2 oranges,
¼ teaspoon of orange zest

For the Raspberry Compote
Juice of 2 oranges
1 cup granulated
sugar
1 lb. raspberries

Preparation:

1. Switch the air fryer to 150°C. Grease a loaf pan.
2. Beat sugar and butter until fluffy. Beat eggs, mashed bananas, lemon zest, buttermilk, and vanilla extract.
3. Add flour, baking soda, and ground cinnamon to the butter mixture.
4. Bake the cake mixture in the air fryer for 30 minutes.
5. When it's cooked, let it cool. Slice into 8 slices.
6. Beat all the ingredients of ricotta frosting for 3-4 minutes. Once done, chill in the fridge.
7. For the raspberry compote, cook raspberries along with orange juice and sugar. Once the syrup thickens, keep it aside and chill.
8. Grill banana bread slices in the air fryer at 85°C.
9. Serve warm slices with ricotta cheese and raspberry compote.

Serving Suggestions: Garnish with fresh raspberries and serve with coffee
Variation Tip: You can use full-fat milk instead of buttermilk.
Per Serving: Calories: 483 | Fat: 20g | Sat Fat: 12g | Carbohydrates: 63g | Fiber: 4g | Sugar: 42g | Protein: 9g

| Chapter 7 Dessert Recipes

Apple Hazelnut Cookies

⏰ **Prep: 10 minutes** 🍱 **Cook: 20 minutes** 📚 **Servies: 6**

Ingredients:

¼ cup butter, plus a little for greasing
1 teaspoon cinnamon
¼ cup raisins
1 cup porridge oats
½ cups pelt flour
2 tablespoons maple syrup
1 cup grated apple
¼ cup unblanched hazelnuts, cut into chunky slices
1 egg

Preparation:

1. Switch the air fryer to 200°C.
2. Grease the air fryer tray with butter and set aside.
3. Microwave butter and syrup together until it is melted.
4. In a saucepan, add melted butter, syrup, and apples. Cook for one minute until it is softened. Add cinnamon and raisins as well.
5. Mix oats, flour, and hazelnuts in a bowl and transfer the cooked apple mixture to that. Beat an egg and combine everything well until the mixture comes together.
6. Scoop out the mixture into the tray and cook for 18 minutes until golden brown.
7. Cook the remaining batch in the same manner.

Serving Suggestions: Serve with cinnamon apple tea.
Variation Tip: You can add almonds as well.
Per Serving: Calories: 146 | Fat: 8g | Sat Fat: 3g | Carbohydrates: 15g | Fiber: 2g | Sugar: 8g | Protein: 2g

Toffee Apple Bread with Cream Pudding

⏰ **Prep: 10 minutes** 🍱 **Cook: 40 minutes** 📚 **Servies: 4**

Ingredients:

3 red dessert apples, cored and diced
Juice of ½ lemon, about 1 tablespoon
4 tablespoons caster sugar
14 oz. can of caramel
6 brioche finger rolls, cut in chunks
3 eggs
1½ cups full-fat milk
1 cup double cream
1 teaspoon vanilla extract

Preparation:

1. Switch the air fryer to 200°C. Preheat for 5 minutes.
2. Toss apples with lemon juice to prevent coloring.
3. Take a deep dish that fits in the air fryer and spread caramel in the base.
4. Layer the chunks of bread and diced apples on top of the caramel. Drizzle more caramel on top.
5. Whisk milk, cream, eggs, sugar, and vanilla with the hand mixer.
6. Pour this mixture on the bread and bake it in the air fryer.
7. It should be firm and brown after 40 minutes.
8. Serve warm.

Serving Suggestions: Serve with vanilla ice cream
Variation Tip: You can add raisins as well.
Per Serving: Calories: 831 | Fat: 37g | Sat Fat: 21g | Carbohydrates: 105g | Fiber: 2g | Sugar: 70g | Protein: 18g

Chapter 7 Dessert Recipes

Orange and Lemon Tangy Pie

⏰ **Prep: 30 minutes**   🍲 **Cook: 20 minutes**   ≋ **Servies: 6**

Ingredients:

11 oz. ready to cook short-crust pastry
For the Filling
1 large egg
4 large egg yolks
14 oz. can of light condensed milk
2 teaspoons lemon juice
⅓ cup orange juice
For the Topping
⅔ cup extra-thick double cream
1 cup Greek yoghurt
4 tablespoons icing sugar

1 teaspoon lemon zest
2 teaspoons of orange zest

more lemon and orange zest to decorate

Preparation:

1. Switch the air fryer to 175°C and preheat for 10 minutes.
2. Roll the pastry and line four tart tins with the pastry.
3. Bake the base in the air fryer for 15 minutes until it turns golden.
4. Whisk egg yolks and egg in a bowl until it turns pale. Add condensed milk along with zests and juices of orange and lemon.
5. Pour in the cooked pastry shells and bake them for 20 minutes in an oven.
6. Once the filling is formed, leave it in the fridge for one hour. You can also leave it in the refrigerator overnight.
7. For the topping, whisk all the topping ingredients until thick. Then, pipe it on the chilled pies.
8. Serve cold.

Serving Suggestions: Garnish with lemon zest and spring flowers.
Variation Tip: You can use low-fat Greek yoghurt as well.
Per Serving: Calories: 647 | Fat: 27g | Sat Fat: 15g | Carbohydrates: 87g | Fiber: 1g | Sugar: 63g | Protein: 12g

Hazelnut Cookies

⏰ **Prep: 25 minutes**   🍲 **Cook: 18 minutes**   ≋ **Servies: 12**

Ingredients:

1 cup hazelnut
½ cup plain flour
1 cup caster sugar
2 eggs
½ teaspoon vanilla extract

Preparation:

1. Switch the air-fryer to 150°C.
2. Mix all the ingredients with an electric mixer until a dough is formed.
3. Line an air fryer tray with parchment paper.
4. Scoop out cookies on the tray and bake for 18 minutes.
5. Once cooked, remove and bake the rest of the dough in batches.

Serving Suggestions: Serve with coffee.
Variation Tip: You can use self-raising flour as well
Per Serving: Calories: 51 | Fat: 2g | Sat Fat: 0g | Carbohydrates: 8g | Fiber: 0g | Sugar: 7g | Protein: 1g

Traditional Cranachan

⏰ **Prep: 15 minutes** 🍲 **Cook: 20 minutes** 🍽 **Servies: 2**

Ingredients:

- 2 cups fresh British raspberries
- 2 tablespoons medium oatmeal
- 1 tablespoon caster sugar
- 1½ cups double cream
- 2 tablespoons honey
- 2-3 tablespoons whisky, to taste

Preparation:

1. Switch the air-fryer to 200°C and preheat for 10 minutes.
2. Toast the oatmeal by air frying it for 20 minutes. It should smell nutty and turn a bit darker in color.
3. For the syrup, blend half of the raspberries and strain through the sieve. Add the caster sugar and mix well.
4. Whisk double cream with whisky and honey. Stir the oatmeal in the cream.
5. Assemble cranachan by layering raspberry sauce, fresh raspberries, and cream mixture.
6. Serve.

Serving Suggestions: serve it chilled.
Variation Tip: You can add roasted walnuts or pecans as well.
Per Serving: Calories: 529 | Fat: 48g | Sat Fat: 27g | Carbohydrates: 18g | Fiber: 2g | Sugar: 13g | Protein: 3g

Banana Cake

⏰ **Prep: 5 minutes** 🍲 **Cook: 40 minutes** 🍽 **Servies: 8**

Ingredients:

For the Topping
- 1½ cup light muscovado sugar
- ½ teaspoon vanilla bean paste
- ½ cup unsalted butter, plus extra for greasing
- 4 large bananas

For the Cake Batter
- 2½ cups plain flour
- 3 large eggs
- ⅔ cup soured cream
- 1 teaspoon cinnamon
- ½ teaspoon ground ginger
- 2 cups golden caster sugar
- ⅔ cup softened unsalted butter
- 2½ teaspoons baking powder

Preparation:

1. Switch the air fryer to 150°C and preheat for 10 minutes.
2. Grease a baking pan with butter.
3. Heat butter, vanilla, and sugar on medium heat until sugar is melted. Pour this caramel sauce into the base of the pan.
4. Cut the bananas lengthwise and arrange them in the base of the cake pan.
5. For the cake batter, beat all the ingredients with the electric mixer until well combined.
6. Pour the batter on top of the bananas and smoothen them out with the spatula.
7. Bake in the air fryer for 40 minutes until the cake is cooked from the center.
8. Remove from the air fryer. Let it cool for some time.
9. Invert the cake into the serving dish and serve.

Serving Suggestions: Serve with egg custard
Variation Tip: You can use dark brown sugar for the base.
Per Serving: Calories: 427 | Fat: 18g | Sat Fat: 11g | Carbohydrates: 62g | Fiber: 2g | Sugar: 45g | Protein: 5g

Coconut Cherry Pie

⏰ **Prep: 15 minutes**   🍲 **Cook: 20 minutes**   🍽 **Servies: 8**

Ingredients:

For Filling
3 cups cherries, pitted and sliced
⅓ cup unsweetened coconut milk

For Topping
¼ cup coconut flour
¼ cup almond flour
¼ cup hemp seeds
1 tsp. ground cinnamon

2 teaspoon almond extract

1 tablespoon. water
2 tablespoons unsalted margarine, softened

Preparation:

1. Switch the air fryer to 190°C and preheat for 10 minutes.
2. Grease a pie dish with butter.
3. In a large bowl, mix together the filling ingredients.
4. Add all topping ingredients in another bowl until a crumbly mixture forms.
5. Fill the prepared pie dish with the mixture.
6. Top with crumb mixture evenly.
7. Bake in the air fryer for approximately 20 minutes. 8. Serve warm.

Serving Suggestions: Serve with ice cream.
Variation Tip: You can use desiccated coconut instead of coconut flour for variation in taste.
Per Serving: Calories: 141 | Fat: 9.2g | Sat Fat: 2g | Carbohydrates: 12.4g | Fiber: 3g | Sugar: 5g | Protein: 2.8g

Easy Gingerbread Bundt Cake

⏰ **Prep: 15 minutes**   🍲 **Cook: 30 minutes**   🍽 **Servies: 6**

Ingredients:

2½ cups all-purpose flour
1 teaspoon salt
1 teaspoon baking soda
1 teaspoon ginger

1 cup molasses
1 large egg
¼ cup granulated sugar
1 cup buttermilk
3 tablespoons butter melted and unsalted

Preparation:

1. Switch the air-fryer to 160°C and preheat for 10 minutes.
2. Mix the flour, salt, ground ginger, and baking soda in a large bowl.
3. Then mix in the egg, buttermilk, molasses, sugar, and butter.
4. Mix well and spray the baking pan with olive oil spray.
5. Let the mixture bake in the air fryer for 30 minutes.

Serving Suggestions: Dust icing sugar while serving.
Variation Tip: You can use mixed spices for variation in taste.
Per Serving: Calories: 320 | Fat: 2g | Sat Fat: 1g | Carbohydrates: 69g | Fiber: 1g | Sugar: 40g | Protein: 6g

Chapter 7 Dessert Recipes

Fluffy Orange Soufflé

⏲ Prep: 5 minutes   🍲 Cook: 10 minutes   🍽 Servies: 6

Ingredients:

3 egg whites
5 tablespoons castor sugar
Orange Curd Filling:
1 egg
1 orange (zest and juice)
3 egg yolks
1 large orange (zest and juice)
2 tablespoons powdered sugar
¼ cup granulated sugar
1 teaspoon cornstarch
2 tablespoons unsalted butter.

Preparation:

1. Preheat your oven to 190°C. Grease 2 ramekins.
2. Mix egg, orange juice, and zest with cornstarch until light and fluffy.
3. Heat butter in a saucepan and add the egg mixture. Mix until the custard thickens. Set it aside and let it cool.
4. Beat egg whites with powdered sugar until fluffy.
5. Beat egg yolks separately with castor sugar until it turns pale. Add orange juice and zest. Fold the egg white and egg yolk mixture gently.
6. Mix the egg mixture with curd and fold gently with a spatula.
7. Add the mixture to the prepared ramekins and bake in the air fryer for 10 minutes.
8. Serve.

Serving Suggestions: Dust with powdered sugar while serving.
Variation Tip: You can add orange extract for a more pungent orangey taste.
Per Serving: Calories: 451 | Fat: 20.7g | Sat Fat: 10.4g | Carbohydrates: 56.5g | Fiber: 2.2g | Sugar: 52.1g | Protein: 13.2g

Pumpkin Pecan Muffins

⏲ Prep: 15 minutes   🍲 Cook: 25 minutes   🍽 Servies: 10

Ingredients:

1½ cups all-purpose flour
1 teaspoon baking soda
1 teaspoon pumpkin pie spice
Pinch of salt
¼ cup maple syrup
3 tablespoons olive oil
3 eggs
1 teaspoon vanilla extract
¾ cup homemade pumpkin puree
¼ cup pecans, chopped

Preparation:

1. Switch the air fryer to 175°C and preheat for 10 minutes.
2. Line a 6-hole muffin tin with the muffin liner.
3. In a large-sized bowl, blend together flour, baking soda, pumpkin pie spice, and salt.
4. In another bowl, add maple syrup, eggs, oil, and vanilla and beat until well blended.
5. Add pumpkin puree and beat until well combined.
6. Add egg mixture and flour mixture together. Mix until well combined.
7. Gently fold in pecans.
8. Place the mixture into prepared muffin cups.
9. Bake for approximately 20-25 minutes.
10. Remove the muffins from the air fryer. Let them cool for about 10 minutes.
11. Serve once cooled.

Serving Suggestions: Serve with cream cheese frosting.
Variation Tip: You can use almond flour instead of all-purpose flour for variation in taste.
Per Serving: Calories: 202 | Fat: 14.6g | Sat Fat: 3g | Carbohydrates: 13.5g | Fiber: 2g | Sugar: 5g | Protein: 3g

Chapter 7 Dessert Recipes | 65

Conclusion

Our journey with the air fryer has been both enlightening and transformative. This amazing appliance is not just about giving a healthier twist to guilty pleasures; it's about reshaping our cooking experience. The recipes serve as mere stepping stones, inviting you to push boundaries, tweak ingredients, and perhaps even pioneer some air-fried masterpieces. Don't be confined by written instructions; the true essence of cooking lies in experimentation and personal touches.

As we wrap up, envision the air fryer as a kitchen gadget and a canvas for future culinary adventures. Its potential is yet to be fully realized, and as the culinary world continues to evolve, so will the wonders of air frying. Remember, every dish you cook adds to this ongoing experience. So, as you enjoy countless healthier and tasty meals, take a moment to celebrate the innovation that the air fryer brings to your kitchen. Continue exploring!

Appendix Recipes Index

A

Air Fryer Chicken Meatballs 45

Air Fryer Curry Chicken Drumsticks 42

Air Fryer Herbed Salmon 33

Air Fryer Kalamansi Tilapia 39

Air Fryer Lemon Mackerel Fillets 38

Air Fryer Mustard Pork Tenderloin 55

Air Fryer Spiced Chicken with Vegetables 47

Air Fryer Steaks with Sweet Potatoes & Mushrooms 51

Apple Hazelnut Cookies 61

B

Baked Lemony Rainbow Trout 39

Banana Bread with Vanilla Ricotta & Raspberries Compote 60

Banana Cake 63

Breakfast Yoghurt Carrot Muffins 12

C

Caramel Chocolate Crumpets with Walnut Praline 15

Cheese Eggplant Rolls 17

Cheese Turkey Meatballs 45

Cheese Vegetable Pie 29

Cheesy Apple and Potato Pasties 21

Cheesy Hash Brown Casserole 19

Chicken and Veggie Skewers 48

Chicken Wings with Blue Cheese Dressing 40

Chicken-Avocado Patties 49

Chili Parsnip and Cauliflower Soup 26

Chocolate and Pear Flapjacks 18

Cinnamon Apple Crisps 23

Cloud Eggs on Toast 14

Coconut Cherry Pie 64

Cream and Cheese Stuffed Pumpkin 27

Cream Carrot Soup with Pancetta Bread 32

Creamy Cauliflower Potato Soup 31

Creamy Fried Squid and Egg Yolks 9

Crispy Air fried Potatoes and Asparagus 17

Crispy Anchovies with Lemon 38

Crispy Breaded Chicken Breasts 44

Crispy Cod 36

Crispy Honey Mustard Halloumi Bars 23

Crispy Parmesan Turkey Cutlets 44

Crispy Spicy Oysters 30

Crispy Tilapia Fillets 36

Crispy Turkey Escalope 43

Cumin Boneless Chicken Thighs 49

D

Delicious Marinated Pork Chops 56

E

Easy Air Fryer Chicken Breasts 47

Easy Air Fryer Lamb Steaks 56

Easy Air Fryer Porterhouse Steaks 51

Easy Air Fryer Salmon 37

Easy Beef Burgers 50

Easy British Mackerel Fillets 28

Easy Gingerbread Bundt Cake 64

Eggy Bread 13

English Breakfast Potato Frittata 15

F

Fluffy Cheese Scones 9

Fluffy Orange Soufflé 65

Fried Oysters with Cheesy Garlic Butter 33

G

Garlicky Cod Loins 37

Garlicky Turkey Breast with Herbs 46

Golden Prawn Balls 22

Green Asparagus Soup 30

Grilled Zucchini Cheese Rolls 25

H

Hazelnut Cookies 62

Herb Roast Beef 54

Herbed Lamb Chops with Garlic Sauce 58

Herbed Lamb Ribs 57

Herbed Steak Bites 50

Homemade Beef Jerky 53

Honey Glazed Salmon 35

Honey Mustard Glazed Chicken Wings 41

L

Lemon Cream Scones 20

M

Macadamia Crusted Rack of Lamb 57

Maple Pears with Roasted Pecan Nuts 60

Marinated Lime Salmon 34

Mini Bean and Sausage Pies with Cheese 21

Mini Cheese Chorizo Frittatas 19

Mini Crumpets Pizza 20

Mustard Pork Chops with Potatoes 54

O

Orange and Lemon Tangy Pie 62

Orange Blueberry Muffins 11

P

Paprika Chicken Thighs 46

Parmesan Carrot Fries 24

Pear, Blackberry and Pistachio Crumble 59

Pesto Egg and Cherry Tomato Muffins 18

Pork Belly with Golden Syrup Sauce 52

Puff Pastry Pigs in a Blanket 22

Pumpkin Pecan Muffins 65

Pumpkin Scones 16

R

Rack of lamb with Mint Pesto 58

Raspberry Cupcakes 59

Roasted Cajun Salmon 34

Roasted Cheese Garlic Dip 26

Roasted Vegetables and Stilton Soup 29

Roasted Vegetables with Herbs 28

Rosemary Vegetable Soup 31

S

Salmon with Tomato Beans Salad 35

Scottish Oats Porridge with Blueberries 14

Scrambled Egg with Fresh Mushrooms 12

Scrambled Eggs with Tomatoes 11

Simple Pork Steaks 55

Simple Turkey Steaks 43

Spiced Chicken with Bird's Eye Chilies 42

Spiced Whole Duck 48

Spicy Butterfly Chicken Drumsticks 41

Spicy Chicken Wings 40

Sticky Beef Bites 24

Sweet & Sour Flank Steak 53

T

Tasty Rib-Eye Steak 52

Toffee Apple Bread with Cream Pudding 61

Tomatoes-Stuffed Peppers with Cheese 27

Traditional Cranachan 63

V

Vanilla Chocolate Banana Bread 13

Vanilla Pumpkin Bread 10

W

Walnut Banana Muffins 10

Printed in Great Britain
by Amazon

Printed in Great Britain
by Amazon